FULFILLMENT HOUR

Fulfilling God's Purposes for the Church
Through the Sunday School Hour

Written by
Jackie S. Henderson and Joan W. Johnson

Edited and Compiled by
George O. McCalep, Jr. Ph.D.

Foreword by
Dr. James T. Draper, Jr.

A Nontraditional Sunday School Model for
Every Denomination and Church

FULFILLMENT HOUR

Unless otherwise indicated, all scripture references and quota-
tions are taken from the Holy Bible, King James Version.

Copyright © 2002 by Orman Press, Inc.
4200 Sandy Lake Drive, Lithonia, GA 30038

ISBN: 1-891773-39-9

Printed in the United States of America

THE FULFILLMENT HOUR MODEL
A Purpose Driven Approach to Sunday School
Based on Matthew 28:19-20, Matthew 22:34–40 and Acts 1:8

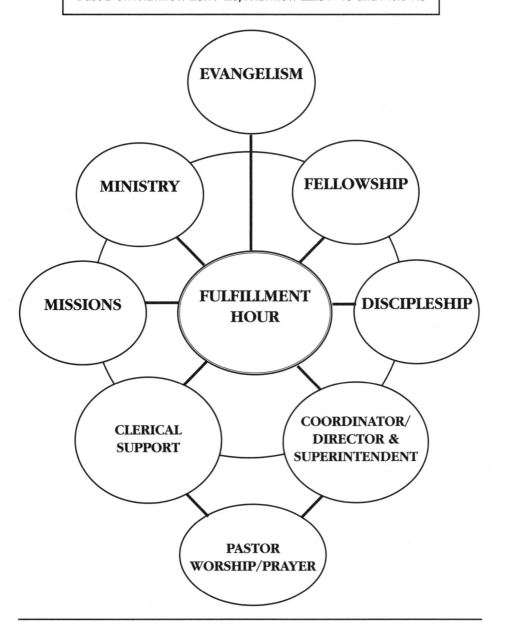

TABLE OF CONTENTS

FOREWORD

The story of Greenforest Community Baptist Church reads like the 29th Chapter of the Book of Acts. It is a continuation of the mighty work of God through the presence and power of the Holy Spirit in the lives of a remarkable group of people. In a miraculous way, God led this church to call Dr. George McCalep, Jr. as pastor. Under his leadership, God has transitioned Greenforest from a small, declining, predominantly Caucasian church to a large, growing, multi-cultural church led by an African American pastor. This church has been a beacon and lighthouse for the Gospel throughout metropolitan Atlanta and around the world. Dr. McCalep has led with grace and vision. He has surrounded himself with leaders who model the servant leadership of our Lord Jesus Christ. And the story breathes with the presence of Jesus and reflects both His glory and His blessings.

"Fulfillment Hour" is about how a church can fulfill all of the purposes and mission of the church through a systematic, balanced and creative approach within the *context* of an hour. This is not a theoretical book of untested ideas. It is a careful presentation of how it is being done and how the same principles can be applied to any church anywhere. Jackie Henderson and Joan Johnson have skillfully articulated this approach.

These pages will challenge, inspire and bless all who read them. I commend it to every individual and church that is serious about ministering to and with the people in our churches. Fulfillment Hour will teach you how to use the time we have available to the greatest advantage. God will bless you as His Spirit reveals fresh, new concepts through this book.

Dr. James T. Draper, Jr.
President, LifeWay Christian Resources

PROLOGUE

WHAT IS FULFILLMENT HOUR?

A Model

Fulfillment Hour is a model in which small groups carry out all of God's biblically mandated purposes of the church during a specific block of time normally assigned to Sunday School. These purposes are:

- Evangelism - Leading people to a belief and greater faith in Jesus Christ.
- Discipleship - Leading people to grow spiritually, live in obedience to God's word and follow Him wholly.
- Fellowship - Leading people to make building godly, loving relationships a priority.
- Ministry/Missions - Leading people to discover their spiritual gifts and use them in edifying the body of Christ.
- Worship - Leading people to express their adoration, honor and love for God.

Fulfillment Hour attempts to fulfill all of the purposes of the church through an organized, balanced approach within the context of an hour, not in an hour, but within the *context* of an hour. It could be said that Fulfillment Hour is a purpose-driven Sunday School. Yet, Fulfillment Hour is much more than Sunday School or another name given to Sunday School. It is a way of "doing church."

The Holy Spirit birthed Fulfillment Hour at the Greenforest Community Baptist Church in Decatur, Georgia. Greenforest has one of the highest numbers of attendees during the traditional 9:45 a.m. Sunday School hour in the country. It is an outgrowth of the Growth-Oriented Sunday School (GOSS) concept. However, it is applicable for all churches and denominations. It is a model that can be duplicated by any church that is willing to change to a new way of thinking about and doing Sunday School.

> *Fulfillment Hour is much more than Sunday School or another name given to Sunday School. It is a way of "doing church."*

Fulfillment Hour is the nucleus, infrastructure and delivery system of the church at work. It focuses the congregation on God's purposes and provides a structure and means for fulfilling them.

The Nucleus

The nucleus is the center of an organic cell and contains material that makes up the organism. It is the blueprint or identity of the organism. The nucleus determines the distinctive identity of the church. Imagine a church with Fulfillment Hour as its nucleonic core. ***A Fulfillment Hour church has a certain blueprint that the church follows for spiritual development and church growth***. As Fulfillment Hour grows, so grows the church. In essence, the church grows through Fulfillment Hour.

The Infrastructure

An infrastructure is the fundamental structure of any system or organization. It is the underlying architecture that determines how well the system functions. Fulfillment Hour gives the church an infrastructure to carry out the purposes of God with ease, flexibility and without duplication of effort.

Fulfillment Hour becomes the main administrative arm of the church for evangelism, discipleship, fellowship, ministry and missions.

Roles and responsibilities relative to carrying out the purposes of the church are assigned primarily to the Fulfillment Hour. Thus, Fulfillment Hour becomes the main administrative arm of the church for evangelism, discipleship, fellowship, ministry and missions. Fulfillment Hour works with the church's ministry leaders to plan, organize, implement and evaluate these functions of the church.

The Delivery System

Delivery involves implementation. The best planning and organizing are in vain if implementation fails. To assure successful implementation, all ministry leaders operate their ministries through the Fulfillment Hour. The advantage of the Fulfillment Hour delivery system is that it puts more people to work carrying out the purposes of the church. For example, Fulfillment Hour has an Evangelism/Outreach Leader for each class who involves the whole class in evangelism instead of the church operating with one minister or director of evangelism and the traditional handful of soul-winners. Thus, Fulfillment Hour is the employment agency of the church.

> The advantage of the Fulfillment Hour delivery system is that it puts more people to work carrying out the purposes of the church.

The Purpose of This Book

This book is designed to provide all of the information needed to implement Fulfillment Hour at any church. It includes all of the details and dynamics to facilitate the implementation process as well as policies, procedures and job descriptions. A great number of forms that have been successfully used at Greenforest are also provided.

Remember, Fulfillment Hour is a model that is supported by a tremendous success story that is still in progress and available for observation. We invite you to read, learn and even visit us at Greenforest. We believe that you, too, will be convinced that implementing the Fulfillment Hour model will take any church to higher levels of spiritual development and church growth.

> *Fulfillment Hour is a model that is supported by a tremendous success story that is still in progress and available for observation.*

THE COMING EXPLOSION
A Perpetual Way of Kingdom Building

"Brethren, be followers together of me, and mark them which walk so as ye have us for an example."—Phil. 3:17

Wow! It's not a fad—here today and gone tomorrow! It's not a symbol of the New Age Movement! It's not a technological advancement that only computer nerds and gurus have the slightest chance of understanding! Instead, it's quite the opposite. It is an explosive model for Sunday School. It is a model for doing church God's way. This simple to understand and implement model is designed for use by any Sunday School of any denomination. It is versatile enough that it can be used by the very small to the very large Sunday School, even by a Sunday School that is just getting off the ground. ***This Sunday School model is called FULFILLMENT HOUR.***

A Deeper Meaning

Fulfillment Hour is what the average church member would refer to as Sunday School. However, its meaning is much deeper. Its goal is far-reaching. Its results are life changing. Jesus said to Philip: "Follow me, and I will make you fishers of men." (Matt. 4:19). Fulfillment Hour is based on following Jesus' example in our walk, in our talk and in our every activity.

> Fulfillment refers to the process of developing Christians who measure up to the will of God.

To get to the real meaning of Fulfillment Hour, we need to break down the word "fulfillment." Webster's Dictionary defines "fulfill" as "to make full; to develop the full potential of; to measure up to." The suffix "ment" refers to "an action or a process." Putting the meanings together gives us fulfillment as "a process of developing potential that measures up." Fulfillment refers to the process of developing Christians who measure up to the will of God.

The "will of God" can be seen in and through the five purposes of the church—evangelism (John 5:28-29), discipleship (Matt. 28:19-20), fellowship (Matt. 25:35-36), ministry/missions (Matt. 22:39-40), and worship (Matt. 22:36-38). Developing these purposes or functions is the major aim of the small, nurturing Bible Study units, which make up Fulfillment Hour. Fulfillment Hour is designed to fulfill all the purposes of the church with the exception of corporate worship. However,

Fulfillment Hour plays a major role in the worship function by preparing the heart. Psalm 34:8 admonishes us to "taste and see that the Lord is good, blessed is the man who takes refuge in Him." Fulfillment Hour is the appetizer for much more to come. It wets the appetite for the main meal—worship.

Fulfillment Hour is an ongoing process that begins on Sunday mornings during the Sunday School hour and lasts all week long. In fact, Fulfillment Hour lasts a lifetime for devoted Christians. It is the catalyst for life-changing growth in the name of our Lord and Savior, Jesus Christ.

The adult and youth Fulfillment Hour classes are organized around the five purposes of the church. Everyone has a position in Fulfillment Hour; not just a position, but a responsibility that has accountability riding on its coattail.

> *Everyone has a position in Fulfillment Hour; not just a position, but a responsibility that has accountability riding on its coattail.*

There are nine ministry positions in the adult and youth Fulfillment Hour classes. They are:

- Shepherd (the Teacher)
- Secretary
- Care Group Leader
- Prayer Leader
- Fellowship Leader
- Discipleship Leader
- Outreach/Evangelism Leader

- Ministry Project Leader
- Missions Leader

The duties for each ministry position are described in Chapters 6–11 and in Appendix 3. Although each ministry position has its own set of duties, those duties often overlap. This is intentional. Fulfillment Hour uses a team approach. The team members work together so that all five purposes of the church are fulfilled.

This goal of Fulfillment Hour is nothing new. Its origin is the Bible, the textbook of Fulfillment Hour. "All Scripture is God-breathed and is useful for teaching, rebuking, correcting and training in righteousness, so that the man of God may be thoroughly equipped for every good work" (2 Tim. 3:16-17). The goal is achieved through a strategy of reaching, sharing and training.

> *Fulfillment Hour vigorously invokes the concept of open enrollment. We are open to enroll anyone, anytime, any place, as a member of Fulfillment Hour, as long as he agrees.*

The Reaching Stage

Fulfillment Hour vigorously invokes the concept of *open enrollment*. Open enrollment means that we are open to enroll anyone, anytime, any place, as a member of Fulfillment Hour, as long as he agrees.

People do not have to be members of the church to be members of Fulfillment Hour; nor do they have to attend a Fulfillment Hour class a certain number of times to be enrolled. They do not even have to be Christians to enroll in Fulfillment Hour. This is a different approach and concept from the traditional Sunday School. ***This is the reaching stage.*** The goal is to get as many people as possible to agree to attend Fulfillment Hour. Our marching order is "to go" (Matt. 28:19). Wherever we go, be it home, school or community, we can enroll

> People do not have to be members of the church to be members of Fulfillment Hour; nor do they have to attend a Fulfillment Hour class a certain number of times to be enrolled. They do not even have to be Christians to enroll in Fulfillment Hour.

Fulfillment Hour members. We can enroll them on the job, at the beauty or barber shop, in the grocery store, on the bus or airplane. We can enroll them any and everywhere. The key is to get permission. The enrollee has to agree to be enrolled in a Fulfillment Hour class. To enroll a preschooler, child or youth, we must first get the parent's or guardian's permission.

We are not focusing on enrollment for the mere purpose of having a large number of learners in attendance in our Fulfillment Hour classes. At the same time, we do not apologize for setting high attendance goals. Every attendee in Fulfillment Hour presents an opportunity to reach a soul for Christ. The more people we have enrolled in Fulfillment Hour, the more people we have in attendance on Sunday. The more people we have in attendance, the more people we expose to learning about Jesus. The more people we expose to learning about Jesus Christ, the more people who are likely to accept Him as

> *The more people we have enrolled in Fulfillment Hour, the more people we have in attendance on Sunday.*

Lord and receive salvation. The more people who accept Jesus and His gift of salvation, the more people there will be who will desire to follow Jesus every day. Wow! What an explosion!

Sharing Jesus

Learning to follow Jesus is exciting and scary, revitalizing and all consuming, as well as motivating and piercing. As we grow in our daily walk with Him, our growing faith in Him turns our fears into unspeakable joy. This joy makes you say and do things you never thought you would. It makes you bold, knowing that you are not alone. "And surely I am with you always, to the very end of the age." (Matt. 28:20) This joy makes you want to follow Him. It makes you want to give your best service. ***It makes you want to share your love of Jesus with others.***

It's a wonderful thing when a believer shares Christ's plan of salvation with a non-believer and then that non-believer prays to receive Christ in his life. This is what Fulfillment Hour teaches. Each Fulfillment Hour class is taught evangelistically. When you teach evangelistically, you pave the way and leave the door open for your learners to see for themselves that the way to eternal life is through Jesus Christ. Thus, prayer and an invitation to receive Jesus Christ is a natural conclusion of a Fulfillment Hour class.

The plan of salvation is shared as often and in as many ways as necessary. The bottom-line is winning souls for Christ. Can you imagine seeing Fulfillment Hour Shepherds walking hand-in-hand down the aisle of the church with new converts who received Christ in their Fulfillment Hour class?

> *Prayer and an invitation to receive Jesus Christ is a natural conclusion of a Fulfillment Hour class.*

As class after class shares Christ and teaches others to share Christ, what an explosion there will be of class members who see the light! Fireworks…Screaming…Crying…Praising…Worshipping…Caring…Loving…Peace…Fireworks of excitement will explode in the heads and hearts of people everywhere as they learn that Jesus loves them and has a wonderful plan for their lives.

Training Stage

Training unlocks the door to an explosive storehouse of gifts and talents. God's people must be properly equipped to carry out His ministry. Initial training is required prior to anyone assuming a Fulfillment Hour leadership position. Ongoing training is used for professional development. Professional development is important because your Fulfillment Hour is going to grow and so will its ministry needs. Also, you do not want your workers to become stale or lose their enthusiasm. Training is an excellent way to share new ideas and keep your workers sharp. (See Chapter 13, "Training is the Key.")

The explosion is coming! There's no doubt about it. God has wonderful rewards in store for His people who remain faithful to Him. If you want to see your church and Sunday School explode, implement the Fulfillment Hour Model.

> *If you want to see your church and Sunday School explode, implement the Fulfillment Hour Model.*

REVAMPING THE TRADITIONAL APPROACH

"Then said he unto them, Therefore every scribe which is instructed unto the kingdom of heaven is like unto a man that is a householder, which bringeth forth out of his treasure things new and old."—Matt. 13:52

"Good morning!" "How are you today?" "It's good to see you!" "How is the family?" There are plenty of hugs, handshakes and "howdy do's" by the grownups, and running and playing by the kids as the small Sunday School crowd gathers in the church. After an acceptable number have arrived, the Sunday School Superintendent rings the bell and calls Sunday School to order.

After a spirit-filled devotion, the Sunday School Superintendent rings the bell again and everyone hurries to his/her Sunday School class for a thorough thirty-minute lecture of the lesson for the day by each Sunday School teacher. Often, the teacher asks students to read from the Sunday School book and explain to the class what they read. After the thirty minutes is over, the Sunday School Superintendent rings the bell for re-assembly. The Pastor or his designee reviews the lesson. The offering for the morning is collected, and the Secretary reads the report for the day—enrollment, attendance and offering. Last Sunday's winners then present attendance and offering banners to this Sunday's winners. Sunday School ends in prayer and everyone is ready for the Sunday morning service.

This traditional Sunday School has been practiced over the years. There's nothing intrinsically wrong with it. It has served our parents, our grandparents, our great grandparents, and on and on very well. However, to quote one of our Fulfillment Hour members, ***"Fulfillment Hour is not my granddaddy's Sunday School."***

God's Expectations

God's expectations for Sunday School are very high. James 3:1 says, "Not many of you should presume to be teachers, my

> Fulfillment Hour has to do with expectations—God's expectations.

brothers, because you know that we who teach will be judged more strictly." Fulfillment Hour has to do with expectations—God's expectations. God expects us to fulfill His purposes for the church through the Sunday School. As stated, His purposes include evangelism, discipleship, fellowship, ministry/mission and worship. The question may be raised, "What is the most effective way to involve the greatest number of believers of any congregation in fulfilling God's biblically mandated purposes?" Because this model is the nucleus, infrastructure and delivery system of the church, "Fulfillment Hour" is the answer.

God also expects us to glorify Him in all that we do. "…Whatsoever ye do, do all to the glory of God." (1 Cor. 10:31) As we are fulfilling His purposes, God expects us to honor and please Him. We are to act as if we were standing right before Him. In Fulfillment Hour, we are conscious of not only what we do, but also how we do it. Everything we do must fulfill God's purposes and glorify Him.

TOSS vs. GOSS

The traditional Sunday School is a teaching-oriented Sunday School (TOSS). Fulfillment Hour is a growth-oriented Sunday School (GOSS). The distinguishing characteristics are:

(1) In the traditional Sunday School, the emphasis is on teaching God's word to believers who are members of the church. GOSS focuses on growing God's kingdom. Therefore, GOSS emphasizes

> *Fulfillment Hour is a growth-oriented Sunday School (GOSS).*

seeking and saving the lost, growing them into Christ-like disciples and sending them out to make more disciples.

(2) TOSS focuses primarily on children, whereas GOSS focuses on adults.

(3) TOSS instruction is focused on the teacher, i.e., what the teacher says and does. GOSS focuses on the learner *learning*.

(4) The Pastor seldom promotes TOSS. In GOSS, the Pastor constantly promotes the Sunday School.

(5) TOSS is an auxiliary of the church while the GOSS is the nucleus of the church.

(6) TOSS is typically found in "Sunday only" churches. GOSS is generally part of a "seven-day-a-week" church.

The Fulfillment Hour Approach

Fulfillment Hour clusters people into age/grade appropriate groups that are organized into classes/units, departments and divisions. Youth and adult groups are organized into classes. The children and preschool groups are structured in units rather than classes. A unit consists of a Shepherd and an assigned group of learners. There may be up to three units in one classroom. (See the example of Greenforest's Fulfillment Hour Organization on page 22.)

Each Fulfillment Hour unit/class is organized to fulfill the purposes of God.

Each Fulfillment Hour unit/class is organized to fulfill the purposes of God. The focus is on both the believer and the unbeliever. The goal is to lead the unbeliever to salvation through faith in our Lord and Savior Jesus Christ, and the believer to be transformed into the likeness and mind of Christ.

In the traditional Sunday School, the positions in the adult Sunday School class are Teacher and Secretary. We have nine primary ministry positions in Fulfillment Hour adult and youth classes. The Shepherd (Teacher) fulfills these roles in the Children's and Preschool divisions. The very abbreviated descriptions of the positions are:

- **Shepherd** - Serves as Bible study leader and administrator of the class while guiding learners toward ongoing spiritual maturity so they can become more like Christ.

- **Secretary** - Maintains class records which includes enrollment, attendance and prospect files; and creates reports based on the record system.

- **Care Group Leader(s)** - Contacts class members on a regular basis through visits, telephone calls, mail, e-mail, etc.

- **Fellowship Leader** - Plans, coordinates and leads social events for the class.

- **Discipleship Leader** - Leads the class in making disciples through formalized discipleship training either as a class or individually.

- **Prayer Leader** - Leads in daily prayer for the needs of members, prospects and the church; encourages members to have personal daily devotional time.

- **Evangelism/Outreach Leader** - Leads Sunday School workers to discover, visit, witness to, enroll, and minister to lost and un-churched prospects.
- **Missions Leader** - Leads the class in serving people who are outside of the congregation by planning, participating in, and/or supporting local, national and international mission projects.
- **Ministry Project Leader** - Leads the class in planning, participating in, and/or supporting ministry projects that serve members of the class or church.

The Fulfillment Hour ministry position leaders lead the class in the work of the church. Members are taught that ministry is service—to the church and each other. Through Fulfillment Hour, members are encouraged to discern their spiritual gifts and find their unique place in the body of Christ. They are guided in

Dividing and sharing the work among the members of the class strengthens all ministries of the church.

discovering where their true passion for service lies so they can be employed in the work of the church. Dividing and sharing the work among the members of the class strengthens all ministries of the church.

Fulfillment Hour is more than a way to organize your Sunday School. Our revamped Fulfillment Hour approach to Sunday School focuses on the fact that ***Sunday School is not JUST about teaching.*** It is a strategy for doing the work of the Great

Commission. Chapters 7–11 explain how the five purposes of the church—evangelism, discipleship, fellowship, ministry and worship—are carried out in Fulfillment Hour.

GREENFOREST COMMUNITY BAPTIST CHURCH
FULFILLMENT HOUR ORGANIZATION

DIVISIONS

1. Adult
2. Youth
3. Children's
4. Preschool

DEPARTMENTS

Adult Division
1. Main Sanctuary
2. Balcony
3. Cornerstone
4. Building 1
5. Building 2
6. Family Life Center
7. Watkins Annex

Youth Division
1. Junior High
   7th Grade
   8th Grade
   9th Grade

2. Senior High
   10th Grade
   11th Grade
   12th Grade

Children's Division
1. 1st Grade
2. 2nd Grade
3. 3rd Grade
4. 4th Grade
5. 5th Grade
6. 6th Grade

Preschool Division
1. 0-12 Months
2. Ones
3. Twos
4. Threes
5. Pre-Kindergarten
6. Kindergarten
7. Pre-First

ADULT/YOUTH CLASSES
CHILDREN/PRESCHOOL UNITS

(Various number of units/classes in each department)

Costs and Rewards

Christian Education is described as that ministry of the church that undergirds all other ministries of the church. Fulfillment Hour is an integral part of Christian Education. In Fulfillment Hour, all of the ministries of the church grow out of the Sunday School.

> *In Fulfillment Hour, all of the ministries of the church grow out of the Sunday School.*

Life experiences have shown us that anything worthwhile costs. Having a nontraditional Fulfillment Hour will call for:

(1) **An Adjustment of Priorities.** Teaching alone is no longer the top priority of the class. The Fulfillment Hour Shepherd (Teacher) is now responsible for caring for the "whole" learner—spiritually, mentally, emotionally and physically. As a result, the lesson plans need to reflect these changes in responsibility.

(2) **More Study Time.** Having an effective Fulfillment Hour requires more study on the part of the leader and the learner. Class preparation is very important. Because the learners are expected to participate more in the class, they are encouraged to study for class.

(3) **Empowerment of Others for Leadership.** Fulfillment Hour encourages learners to discover their spiritual gifts and then put their gifts into service.

Additionally, each adult class is encouraged to "twin" or duplicate itself, which means constantly training individuals to fulfill leadership roles. For example, as Preschool, Children's and Youth Fulfillment Hour units outgrow their space, new units with new leaders should be created.

(4) More Involvement in Spiritual Development. Fulfillment Hour encourages all participants to strive toward personal growth and spiritual development beyond the Fulfillment Hour lesson. This may mean attending Bible study classes or discipleship lessons outside of the regular class hour.

(5) Constant Management. Fulfillment Hour requires constant management. This includes managing people, materials, records and space. Leaders must be assigned and trained for each class/unit. Records must be kept current. This includes the Sunday School roll, prospect list, individual member records and division/department/class records. Records strengthen ministry because they tell you where you have been, where you are and where you need to improve. Space should be managed so that the maximum attendance is consistent with the room size and leader/learner ratio. (See Appendix 11, Meeting

Space Specifications Chart.) As you manage each of these areas, it is important to remain focused on reaching people for Christ. You must ensure that people grow spiritually, as well as numerically.

(6) Constant Promotion. Fulfillment Hour must be constantly before the congregation. The Pastor should say something about Fulfillment Hour every Sunday from the pulpit. This allows the membership to see the importance of Fulfillment Hour. Other promotional resources include banners, signs, fliers, e-mails, letters, etc.

(7) Constant Encouragement. Each division/department/class has to be encouraged in the form of recognition and praise. Let the people know that not only are they good, but they are the best. Help them believe that they are better than they think they are. Give recognition regularly. Every gathering is an opportunity to recognize and encourage those who do the work. At Greenforest, we give recognition in our Weekly Workers' Meetings, in the classroom, and at the Annual Appreciation Banquet. (See Appendix 22.)

(8) Constant Leadership Development. *There are no trained leaders, only leaders in training.* Leadership development has to be ongoing. Leaders must develop personally, professionally and spiritually. Fulfillment Hour focuses on developing leadership skills so that all leaders can become all that God has intended them to be.

While the costs may seem high, the benefits are even greater. Having a nontraditional Fulfillment Hour will help your church:

- Grow spiritually.
- Increase the number of people receiving Christ.
- Open the front doo.r
- Close the back door.
- Enhance the worship experience.
- Involve more people in ministry.
- Increase offerings.

THE NEED AND CERTAINTY OF CHANGE

"And be not conformed to this world: but be ye transformed by the renewing of your mind, that ye may prove what is that good, and acceptable, and perfect, will of God."—Romans 12:2

C hange is a natural part of life for all of us. In order to grow, there must be change. God is continually doing something fresh and new in our lives. God brings about change in us as believers. As a result, ***Fulfillment Hour is an instrument of change.***

This chapter is about changing our attitude about Sunday School to be like the hymn: "I'm pressing on the upward way, new heights I'm gaining every day. Still praying as I'm onward bound. Lord lead me on to higher ground." No longer can we think of Sunday School as a "once-a-week" experience on Sunday morning. The Sunday School must change to become the nucleus, the infrastructure and the delivery system of the church.

Implementation of Change

Sunday School leaders everywhere become very excited when they attend our workshops and learn how they can not only grow their Sunday School, but also grow their churches. They become energized, begin setting goals and start putting ideas on paper. The problem arises when they go back to their churches and present their new ideas. Total frustration soon develops because the church's status quo group naturally resists change. If this happens to you, don't give up! Resistance is normal when something new is introduced. Fast and pray for the Holy Spirit to open their hearts and minds. Then push for change. "Be strong and of good courage, fear not, nor be afraid of them: for the Lord thy God, He it is that doth go with thee; He will not fail thee nor forsake thee." (Deut. 31:6)

> *Make deliberate changes that strategically support the principles of Fulfillment Hour.*

What to Change

You will not make changes just for the sake of change. Instead, you will make deliberate changes that strategically support the principles of Fulfillment Hour. Some of the changes you will want to implement are:

- **Change the name of your Sunday School to Fulfillment Hour.** Make sure your congregation knows that the Sunday School's new mission is to fulfill God's five purposes for the church. You may also consider using *Shepherd* instead of Teacher. Fulfillment Hour Shepherds do much more than teach. They are responsible for the total needs of the sheep God has entrusted to them.

- **State your new philosophy of Sunday School in a Fulfillment Hour vision statement.** Once it's in writing, share it with the congregation and display it prominently. The vision statement for Fulfillment Hour at Greenforest is "to build a community of small Bible study units whose members develop relationships through fellowship and study as they daily and devoutly love, follow and model Christ."

- **Implement the *Ten Best Practices to Make Your Sunday School Work* by Ken Hemphill and Bill Taylor.** These best practices give you a basic outline from which you can develop strategies for implementation.

  (1) Commit to the Strategy (Col. 3:23-24). Leaders must commit to the Fulfillment Hour model and the process of change. They must also have a mindset that welcomes change.

  (2) Organize with Purpose (Mark 5:39, 41-42). Don't just structure your Fulfillment Hour into divisions, departments and classes. Organize it to fulfill the purposes of God (see divisional organizational charts in Appendix 2) and then, make sure everyone knows and understands the purposes that they are fulfilling.

(3) **Build Kingdom Leaders (Mark 10:43-45).** As the kingdom grows, more leaders will be needed. Multiply and grow your Fulfillment Hour leaders. Train them for effectiveness in all five functions of the church. (See training ideas in Chapter 13.)

(4) **Develop Soul-Winners (2 Tim. 2:1-2).** Train your leaders to be soul-winners who are accountable. See enrollment as a ministry opportunity. Contact and invite people to Fulfillment Hour through outreach by using cards, calls, visits, e-mail, etc. Be constantly conscious of inviting people to Fulfillment Hour everywhere you go. Then, use attendance records to inspect what you expect. Ask each member of the class to report weekly on the number of times he/she shared Christ, how many people received Christ and the number of contacts made. (See Appendix 15 for a sample Attendance Record.)

(5) **Win the Lost (Rom. 19:13-14).** A soul-winning consciousness must be before class members at all times. Soul-winning consciousness means knowing

the spiritual status of each member in his or her class. Teach every Fulfillment Hour lesson evangelistically. Don't assume that everyone present is saved. In worship service, the messenger always closes by talking about Jesus. The adult and youth class leader should give the plan of salvation at the end of every lesson.

(6) **Assimilate People (1 Cor. 12:12-14).** Have a plan in place to enroll new members in Fulfillment Hour as they join the church.

(7) **Partner with Families (Psalm 78:4, 6).** The church and families are partners in training our children. Host programs that bring preschool parents and Shepherds together to discuss issues that affect the rearing of their children. Our Preschool Division conducts a "Family Matters Seminar" quarterly.

(8) **Teach to Transform (Phil. 4:9).** Using the Bible as your textbook, teach to move people beyond information and inspiration to transformation. Being transformed into the likeness of Christ should be every believer's goal. (See Chapter 4, "The Role Leadership.")

(9) **Mobilize for Ministry (Matt. 25:37).** Have a Ministry Project Leader and a plan for ministry projects in every Fulfillment Hour class. Meeting the

personal needs of people is how we strengthen the body of Christ so it can fulfill the other purposes of the church. Regardless of your Fulfillment Hour structure, always have a Ministry Project leader. (See Shepherds' responsibility in Appendix 3.)

(10) Multiply Leaders and Classes/Units (Acts 13:2-3). Involve class members in setting goals related to "twinning" (duplicating) their class. (See "Twinning" in Chapter 12.) God's kingdom is expanded when new leaders and new units/ classes are created.

Resistance to Change

Resistance to change is a natural and inevitable reaction to the disruption of normal expectations. In Dr. George O. McCalep, Jr.'s book, *Faithful Over a Few Things*, he gives the ten most common reasons why people resist change:

> *Resistance to change is a natural and inevitable reaction to the disruption of normal expectations.*

(1) It makes people feel out of control. People tighten up when they feel powerless.

(2) There is too much uncertainty. What will it mean for them? Is it safe?

(3) They have never heard it before. People do not respond well when asked for a reaction on the spot. The ground must first be prepared.

(4) It disrupts routine. The known and certain are appealing.

(5) It makes people lose face. It seems as if what they did in the past was wrong.

(6) It makes people feel uncertain about their competence.

(7) It disrupts other things. There is a ripple effect on other people and their efforts.

(8) Things that are new require more work. People feel they have no reason to put in the extra effort.

(9) They have a chip on their shoulder from the past. People are angry because of something else.

(10) Sometimes the threat is real. The great idea will hurt someone else.

Dynamics of Change

The following are some dynamics to remember when leading people to change:

- People can only handle so much change at once. Just as you eat an elephant a bite at a time, implement your Fulfillment Hour in digestible phases.

- People feel awkward and self-conscious because change takes them out of their comfort zones.
- People think first about what they have to give up. You must constantly keep the vision of the benefits and rewards in front of them.
- People feel alone when in the midst of change. They will need to be reminded that Jesus is with them throughout the entire implementation process and thereafter.
- People will be convinced that they don't have enough resources. Help them to know that God is able to meet all their needs.
- People are at different levels of readiness. People adapt to change differently even though they know change is going to happen. Pray for the Holy Spirit to help them through the process. Ask the Holy Spirit to bear in you the fruit of patience and long-suffering. You will have to love them through the change.
- People will revert back to their old behavior when under stress. This is a natural reaction, but it is not godly. We are new creatures. However, the new Spirit in us must be fed and strengthened by constantly renewing our minds.

Where Do We Start?

Step 1: Pray.

As with any and everything associated with Fulfillment Hour, it all begins with prayer. It is true, "prayer changes people." Anything worth having is worth going to God in prayer. James 4:2 states, "...ye have not because ye ask not." To have an effective Fulfillment Hour, you must first pray to discern God's

> As with any and everything associated with Fulfillment Hour, it all begins with prayer.

will for your church, and then for the hearts of the people to be changed from criticizing, complaining and condemning to committed, compassionate and courageous. Next, pray for God to send people who are equipped with the spiritual gifts needed to fill every position. Finally, pray continuously throughout the entire process. 1 Thessalonians 5:17 tells us to "Pray without ceasing."

Step 2: Enlist the Pastor.

The strongest ministry for carrying out the Great Commission is Fulfillment Hour and *the most powerful person to promote Fulfillment Hour is the Pastor.* The Pastor should mention Fulfillment Hour from the pulpit on a regular basis, encouraging the congregation to enroll in and attend Fulfillment Hour regularly. The worship hour has the largest group of people. If nothing is said in the worship hour about Fulfillment Hour, people will develop an attitude that Fulfillment Hour is not important and they do not need to attend. The Pastor should also participate in Fulfillment Hour. (See "Ten Ways to Help Your Pastor Become a Fulfillment Hour Pastor" in Appendix 1.)

Step 3: Create the vision.

Talk with the Pastor and the church ministry leaders about their programs and the vision they have for your church. Work with them to determine how the Fulfillment Hour model can be used to employ people to support the church's ministries, particularly evangelism, discipleship, outreach, missions, fellowship and worship.

Step 4: Communicate the vision.

The congregation needs to know and understand that the Sunday School is changing its focus from teaching to fulfilling God's purposes. Their minds and hearts must be prepared so that they will commit to fulfilling God's purposes for the church. Fulfillment Hour then becomes an organized and direct way of acting upon their commitment.

> *The congregation needs to know and understand that the Sunday School is changing its focus from teaching to fulfilling God's purposes.*

Five things should be regularly said about Fulfillment Hour during the worship service (based on the Parable of the Lost Sheep found in Luke, Chapter 15):

(1) Specific programs or ministries Fulfillment Hour is supporting (the mission of the flock)

(2) Total enrollment (a shepherd had 100 sheep)

(3) Attendance (missing sheep discussed)

(4) Number of visits and/or contacts made last week (ways to find missing sheep)

(5) Number of new members that joined on Sunday (acknowledgement of found sheep)

Step 5: Develop a plan to manage the change process.

People adapt to change differently even when they know in advance that a change is going to happen. Knowing that you will have people with varying levels of acceptance to this new approach to Sunday School, it is prudent to have a plan in place that will allow you to reach everyone where they are.

There are those who initiate change and those who respond to change. We know that you are an initiator because you are reading this book. Your concern is how to help others respond positively to Fulfillment Hour. You must realize that implementing Fulfillment Hour inherently creates resistance because it challenges your congregation's values, emotions, knowledge, behavior, bases of control, politics, logistics and economics. However, through Spirit-filled compassion and God-given agape love, you will be able to love them through the change process.

You will work with three primary groups of people as you implement Fulfillment Hour:

- **Sponsors:** Those who can legitimize the change. (Example: Pastor and Church Ministry Leaders)
- **Implementers:** The people who will work with you to establish Fulfillment Hour.
- **Target Group:** The people who will actually have to change what they have been doing. They include the existing superintendent, secretary, teachers, Sunday School class members and the rest of the congregation.

> *Implementing Fulfillment Hour inherently creates resistance because it challenges your congregation's values, emotions, knowledge, behavior, bases of control, politics, logistics and economics.*

Within each group you will have advocates (cheerleaders) who believe in the need to change to Fulfillment Hour and want it to happen in your church. As you work with each of the aforementioned groups, identify your cheerleaders early so they can help communicate and sustain the vision through the implementation process.

Develop a plan to manage the change to Fulfillment Hour. Create a plan that will help each group move from awareness of Fulfillment Hour to acceptance, adoption, institutionalization and finally internalization. Begin by anticipating each group's questions, concerns and fears. Then, list how Fulfillment Hour will benefit them. Your plan should build commitment. It should be a plan that:

- **Provides accurate and complete information throughout the implementation process.** Work to eliminate confusion and build understanding. Do not assume that awareness of Fulfillment Hour is the same as understanding the nature and intent of the change.

> Develop a plan to manage the change to Fulfillment Hour. Create a plan that will help each group move from awareness of Fulfillment Hour to acceptance, adoption, institutionalization and finally internalization.

- **Involves lots of people in planning and implementation. Involvement is the key to commitment.** People are more likely to commit to something when they have invested time and energy. Involvement leads to ownership.

- **Rewards people for their participation.** Everyone wants to be appreciated and recognized for his/her efforts.

- **Supports changing emotions.** Those who perceive the change to Fulfillment Hour negatively typically move through phases of passivity, shock, immobility, anger, depression, testing and, finally, acceptance.

Those who perceive the change to Fulfillment Hour positively may start out with certainty, but then become doubtful as they learn more about what it involves. You want their doubts to turn into hope, which leads to confidence and, ultimately, satisfaction with the change to Fulfillment Hour.

It may sound like a lot, but don't worry. God will grant you the ability to remain faithful and steadfast so you can hang in there when the going gets tough. He will also give you the courage to stand tall and be bold as the enemy, Satan, attacks. Most of all, He will enable you to love those who catch the vision, as well as those who resist your efforts at every turn.

Step 6: Organize the Fulfillment Hour Administrative Staff.

The Fulfillment Hour Administrative Staff plans, conducts and evaluates the work of the Fulfillment Hour. The number of people and positions needed to administer your Fulfillment Hour will vary depending on the size of your congregation. At the very least, you will need a Superintendent, Secretary, and Coordinator/Director for each age-level division. You may also need Department Directors if your divisions are large enough to be divided into multiple departments. ***The overwhelming concern is not what job titles to use, but the selection of godly people who will fully commit to carrying out God's purposes through Fulfillment Hour.*** (See Chapter 5, "Getting Organized.")

Step 7: Fill the ministry positions.

"Ask and ye shall receive." Ask God to send people with the spiritual gifts you need. He will send people who are filled with His Spirit, passionate about fulfilling His purposes, and committed to Fulfillment Hour.

All Fulfillment Hour leaders should meet the following qualifications:

(1) Have received Jesus Christ and are assured of their salvation. (Rom. 10:13)

(2) Be **FATTER**:

F - Faithful: Believing, full of faith, firm in attendance to promise, true to God and His church. (1 Cor. 4:1-2; Luke 9:57-62; Matt. 6:33)

A - Available: Accessible for use, at hand, usable. (Matt. 6:33)

T - Teachable: Capable of being taught and willing to learn. (Acts 2:42)

T - Tither: Pays at least the tenth as a starting point in their giving. (Mal. 3:8-10; James 1:7)

E - Enthusiastic: Excited, eager, motivated. (Acts 2:46-47)

R - Reproducible: Willing to share with and invest their God-given knowledge and experience in someone else. (II Tim. 2:2)

(3) Have a stable personal life.

(4) Completed the training courses that are required for the position.

In conclusion, we must change our way of thinking about Sunday School. It is not just for children. It is for all ages. What's more, it is a strategy to grow the church spiritually and numerically. Have the courage to carry out the Great Commission through your own Fulfillment Hour. Acts 1:8 gives us the courage and the power to make change a reality. Don't be afraid. Make the decision to change your Sunday School to Fulfillment Hour today.

> *We must change our way of thinking about Sunday School. It is not just for children. It is for all ages. What's more, it is a strategy to grow the church spiritually and numerically.*

THE ROLE OF LEADERSHIP

"I beseech you therefore, brethren, by the mercies of God, that ye present your bodies a living sacrifice, holy, acceptable unto God, which is your reasonable service."—Romans 12:1

Fulfillment Hour recognizes that the leader is a lesson. Servant leaders should be examples of Christianity in their personal living. In order for the Fulfillment Hour model to work, the church's leadership must be on board. This begins with the pastor. The pastor is the key to making it happen. The church leadership must see and know that Fulfillment Hour is a top priority for the Pastor. The church membership must see and know that Fulfillment Hour is a top priority for the church leadership. (See "Ten Ways to Help Your Pastor Become a Fulfillment Hour Pastor" in Appendix 1.) Fulfillment Hour's success depends heavily upon the acceptance of and implementation by the church leadership.

Rev. John D. Ogletree, Jr., pastor of the First Metropolitan Church in Houston, Texas, facilitated a workshop entitled "Leading and Managing Change in the Congregation." Rev.

Ogletree shared that the rules of leadership have changed over time. Some of the changes are:

Old Rule	New Rule
Faithfulness is sufficient.	Effectiveness is expected.
Ministry depends on the leader.	Ministry depends on the team.
Godliness is assumed but not required.	Godliness is required but not assumed.

One of the challenges facing organizations is continuing their growth. The essence of growth is change. When leadership chooses to remain the same despite changing circumstances and a changing environment, the organization begins to die a "slow death." To eliminate falling into this status quo trap, Fulfillment Hour steps in, rejuvenates and revitalizes the leaders of the church and Sunday School.

> To eliminate falling into this status quo trap, Fulfillment Hour steps in, rejuvenates and revitalizes the leaders of the church and Sunday School.

The role of the Fulfillment Hour leadership is to fulfill the purposes of God through the time frame traditionally given to Sunday School. Ken Hemphill and Bill Taylor's book, *Ten Best Practices to Make Your Sunday School Work*, states that "the Sunday School calls leaders to a prophetic ministry, one in which they listen to God's voice, discover His message, integrate His message into their lives and proclaim His truth through His church to the nations."

Transformational Leadership

The expected outcome of Fulfillment Hour is ***changed lives that model Christ.*** Jesus displayed His love in all that He did. We are to follow His example. Our transformed lives should constantly demonstrate love for God and others.

Transformed Fulfillment Hour leaders must model for the learners that "God is love" and "God is truth." Philippians 4:9 states, "Whatever you have learned or received or heard from me, or seen in me—put into practice. And the God of peace will be with you."

> *The expected outcome of Fulfillment Hour is changed lives that model Christ.*

Ken Hemphill and Bill Taylor wrote, "The Sunday School teacher and all other Sunday School leaders must model the truth that God transforms lives day-by-day. The leaders must move beyond being content with transferring biblical information and calling for discussions about application to walking with their learners in obedient, Christ-centered living." Fulfillment Hour leaders are given the task of setting the standard for the church. This standard places Fulfillment Hour in the role of moving ministry to the next level.

With the vision of Fulfillment Hour, comes the new name for the teacher, *Shepherd.* This new name brings new responsibilities. The major responsibility of the teacher is to teach, but the Shepherd also counsels, encourages, disciplines and guides the learners to transformed lives. The Fulfillment Hour Shepherd has a major leadership responsibility.

> With the vision of Fulfillment Hour, comes the new name for the teacher, "Shepherd." This new name brings new responsibilities.

Dr. David Tiller and Larry Garner in *Teaching Like Jesus* share that there are nine theological principles for spiritual transformation. Transformational leaders adhere to all nine of the following principles:

(1) The will of God is that believers will ultimately be transformed into the image of Jesus.

(2) Spiritual transformation is the work of God.

(3) Spiritual transformation is an internally driven process not an externally driven process.

(4) Although an internal process, spiritual transformation has external results.

(5) While related, spiritual transformation and spiritual maturity are not synonymous.

(6) Spiritual transformation continues until believers see God—either at death or at the coming of Christ.

(7) The individual must yield to the work of the Spirit for transformation to occur.

(8) Teachers do not engineer spiritual transformation, create it or cause it to happen.

(9) We do not know exactly when, where or by what means God will generate spiritual transformation.

One of our core beliefs about Fulfillment Hour is that the identification and awareness of each member's passion and spiritual gifts for ministry is the key to effective ministry and mission productions. Therefore, men and women with appropriate leadership gifts should lead the church. Leadership is a spiritual gift from God. The Fulfillment Hour Administration spends a great amount of time and energy enlisting leaders. The Fulfillment Hour leadership is highly effective when proper enlistment begins, ends and continues in prayer. Before the Administration can match individuals' spiritual gifts and passions with positions, the individuals must know what their spiritual gifts and passions are. Tiller and Garner wrote, "If an individual is working within his spiritual gift, he won't have to worry about being burned out—God provides a freshness, a renewal, a brand new walk that allows him to go that extra mile."

In addition, Henry T. Blackaby reveals in *Christianity: A Follower's Guide*, "An ordinary person is who God most likes to use." Paul said God deliberately seeks out the weak things and the despised things because it is from them that he can receive the greatest glory (1 Cor. 1:26-31). Then everyone will know that only God could have done it. ***If you feel weak, limited or***

ordinary, you are the best material through which God can work!

The Christian faith is grounded in transformation (changed lives). Fulfillment Hour concurs. Leaders must be anointed to carry out the task of change. The key to initiating change is effective leadership. For Fulfillment Hour to be successful, its transformed leaders must be willing and able to initiate change as a prerequisite to fulfilling God's will.

> *For Fulfillment Hour to be successful, its transformed leaders must be willing and able to initiate change as a prerequisite to fulfilling God's will.*

"Moreover thou shalt provide out of all the people able men, such as fear God, men of truth, hating covetousness; and place such over them, to be rulers of thousands, and rulers of hundreds, rulers of fifties, and rulers of tens."—Exodus 18:21

ulfillment Hour is a people intense ministry. It requires strong, godly leadership to coordinate the people, space, materials and records. Just as Jethro advised Moses to select God-fearing men to help him judge matters for the people, we recommend a team of godly leaders to administer Fulfillment Hour.

Fulfillment Hour falls under the Christian Education Ministry of the church. If your church has a Minister/Director of Christian Education, then he/she will be responsible for Fulfillment Hour. However, we recognize the need for flexibility in structuring your Fulfillment Hour. If your church does not have a Minister/Director of Christian Education, then the

Superintendent will fulfill the responsibilities we have listed for the Minister/Director of Christian Education.

The number of Fulfillment Hour staff positions you have will depend on the size of your congregation and the number of Fulfillment Hour classes you have to manage. Generally your organizational structure will include the folowing positions:

- Minister/Director of Christian Education
- Superintendent
- Assistant Superintendent
- Secretary
- Coordinator/Directors (for each age-level division)

When your age-level divisions grow to the point where they need to be divided into multiple departments, you will need to add Department Directors to help manage the additional administrative responsibilities. The need to create departments may be driven by the number of classes (enrollment) in a division or by location. The adult departments at Greenforest grew out of the need to manage classes in multiple buildings. The departments in the Preschool, Children's and Youth divisions, which are based on age/grade levels, grew with our enrollment.

You can be certain that your Fulfillment Hour will grow your church. When your church grows to the point that you have full-time Ministers of Evangelism, Discipleship, Missions and Social Services, you may consider adding members to the

Fulfillment Hour Administrative Staff to act as liaisons to the ministers in each of these areas. The liaisons will communicate the strategies and priorities of the church ministry leaders to the Fulfillment Hour Administration and help implement those strategies through Fulfillment Hour.

The following are general descriptions of the Fulfillment Hour Administrative Staff positions. (See Appendix 3 for complete position descriptions.)

Minister/Director of Christian Education

The Minister/Director of Christian Education oversees Fulfillment Hour and reports directly to the Pastor. He/she works with the Superintendent, Assistant Superintendent and all age-level Coordinator/Directors in planning, conducting and evaluating the work of the Fulfillment Hour. The Minister/Director of Christian Education works to support all church ministries by ensuring that the church's strategies for carrying out God's purposes are effectively implemented through Fulfillment Hour. His/her responsibilities include:

- Implementing and supporting the Fulfillment Hour model.
- Regularly communicating with the Pastor, Church Ministry Leaders and Fulfillment Hour Coordinator/Directors to ensure all efforts are successfully coordinated and quality is maintained.

- Ensuring that workers are properly enlisted and trained.
- Providing direction in the selection of curriculum materials.
- Directing others in the proper use of curriculum materials.

Superintendent

This position is different from the traditional Sunday School in many ways. The Superintendent works with the Minister/Director of Christian Education and Assistant Superintendent in planning, conducting and evaluating the work of the Fulfillment Hour. He/she is specifically responsible for:

- Implementing and supporting the Fulfillment Hour model.
- Developing and maintaining the Weekly Workers' Meeting.
- Ensuring that a Shepherd is in place for every class/unit.
- Enlisting substitute Shepherds or being prepared to fill-in, when needed.
- Providing support and guidance to other staff members in accomplishing their work.

Assistant Superintendent

The Assistant Superintendent assists the Superintendent and the Minister/Director of Christian Education in planning, conducting and evaluating the work of Fulfillment Hour. The Assistant Superintendent is primarily responsible for assimilating new members into Fulfillment Hour and providing backup support to the Superintendent. Some of the specific tasks the Assistant Superintendent may perform are:

- Escorting guests and new members to classes.
- Coordinating Fulfillment Hour tours for new members.
- Filling in for the Superintendent in leading the Weekly Workers' Meeting, when needed.

Secretary

The Secretary's role is very important because this position tracks all of the Fulfillment Hour metrics of measurement (statistics). The Secretary is responsible for compiling and maintaining the records that are reported weekly from each Fulfillment Hour class/unit. These metrics are vital to measuring growth, knowing where you are in each critical area and determining where you need to focus attention.

The actual record-keeping system may vary depending upon the size of the congregation and available resources of the church. Whether a church uses forms that are manually updated or an elaborate, computer-generated program is not the main concern. The main concern is that a record-keeping system is used and updated regularly for Fulfillment Hour. Properly maintained records will provide the administration with the enrollment and attendance in each class, unit, department and division. You can readily see what is happening in the lives of members of the Fulfillment Hour from properly maintained records.

Coordinator/Director

In Fulfillment Hour, the Coordinator/Director is another name for the Divisional Director. The divisions are Adult, Preschool, Children's and Youth. There should be a Coordinator/Director for each division. Coordinator/Directors lead in determining the Fulfillment Hour organization needed to effectively reach and teach their age-level division. The Coordinators/Directors are responsible for coordinating activities, conducting training and ensuring quality for their divisions. Their duties include:

- Inspecting their respective divisions on Sunday mornings to be sure that classes and Shepherds are in place, and that the Fulfillment Hour model is being followed.
- Providing ongoing training to their Shepherds during the divisional breakouts in the Weekly Workers' Meetings.

- Giving direction in the selection and proper use of age-level curriculum materials.
- Assigning mentors to work with new Shepherds.
- Communicating with the Fulfillment Hour Administration on a weekly basis to ensure quality.

Department Director

The effort that is required to communicate with your Shepherds and track statistics will also grow as your Fulfillment Hour grows. The task of disseminating and collecting information is made manageable by having Department Directors to assist the Secretary. The Department Directors also help to manage the Fulfillment Hour classes on Sunday mornings. Their roles differ depending of the age-level division they support.

Department Director – Adult Division

The Department Director's role in the Adult Division is very different from those in the Preschool, Children's and Youth Divisions. Because the Adult Division Shepherds work autonomously, the Adult Division Department Director primarily distributes and collects the weekly Attendance Records and disseminates information to the Shepherds. If the Administration needs information from the Shepherds, the Department Directors will help collect the information and return it to the Fulfillment Hour office.

The Adult Division Department Director also becomes another set of eyes and ears for the Superintendent. The Department Director is often the first to recognize a problem on Sunday morning, e.g., a Shepherd is delayed in arriving or the heat is not working in a particular classroom. We rely on the Department Directors to report any problem to the Administration and, if necessary, assist in resolving it.

Department Director – Preschool, Children's and Youth Divisions

Department Directors are recommended in the Preschool, Children's and Youth divisions whenever there are two or more Shepherds with classes/units for the same age/grade level. In our Preschool and Children's divisions, we maintain a ratio of six learners to every one Shepherd (6:1). We may have up to three Shepherds in a single room. Each room has three tables with a Shepherd and six children at each table. Each table is a "unit." The Department Director is responsible for all units within a specific age/grade.

The Department Director in the Preschool, Children's and Youth Divisions plays an active role in the classroom each Sunday. When a child enters the room, the Department Director greets the child and directs him/her to a learning station with pre-planned activities or to the assigned Shepherd. The Department Director helps the Shepherds carry out the learning activities for the lesson during class. At the end of class, they collect the weekly Attendance Records. If a Shepherd is absent, the Department Director may teach, if necessary.

Division/Department Secretary

Another way of helping the Fulfillment Hour Secretary manage the enrollment records and track the statistics on a division/department level is by having Secretaries for each division and department. Division/Department Secretaries are optional. We recommend doing what is most effective for your Fulfillment Hour.

THE ROLE OF THE SHEPHERD

"And Jesus, when He came out, saw much people, and was moved with compassion toward them, because they were as sheep not having a shepherd." —St. Mark 6:34

The Shepherd's role is to care for God's sheep. ***The Shepherd (Teacher) is the leader of the sheep (Fulfillment Hour class members).*** The Shepherd leads the sheep toward spiritual maturity and transformation by providing experiences that will develop disciples. In John 21:15-17, Jesus asked Peter if he loved Him three times. Each time, Peter assured Jesus that he loved Him. "Yea, Lord; thou knowest that I love thee." (John 21:15) The first time Jesus said, "Feed my lambs." After the second and third time Peter replied, Jesus responded, "Feed my sheep." The message to us is clear. If we love Jesus, we will nurture and care for His people, both the saved and unsaved.

The Shepherd's Role

The Shepherd has the awesome responsibility of ministering to God's people. He or she is very much like a Pastor, nurturing a flock while ensuring that individual needs are met. The Shepherd cares for the whole learner helping to meet spiritual, mental, emotional and physical needs. In so doing,

> *The Shepherd cares for the whole learner helping to meet spiritual, mental, emotional and physical needs.*

the Shepherd is the leader and model for the class in Bible study, evangelism, discipleship, fellowship, missions/ministry and worship. The Shepherd's key responsibilities are to:

- Know every member of the class personally.
- Involve the class in fulfilling all five of God's purposes for the church.
- Teach God's word.
- Minister to the personal needs of the class members.
- Grow more Fulfillment Hour leaders.
- Model what it means to be a devoted follower of Christ.
- Strive to be a better Shepherd through ongoing personal and professional development.
- Fulfill administrative duties.

The Shepherd's Duties

There are specific duties associated with each of the Shepherd's key responsibilities. The following describes the duties or tasks that must be carried out to effectively fulfill each responsibility:

- **Know every member of the class personally.**
  - Know each member of the unit/class by name.
  - Ensure that a class member contacts each member of the unit/class weekly.
  - Ensure that the Shepherd contacts each member of the unit/class quarterly (whether absent or not).
- **Involve the class in fulfilling all five of God's purposes for the church.**
  - Enlist leaders for all class positions and make sure they are properly trained.
  - Fulfill the duties of each class position that is not filled.
  - Ensure that the Evangelism/Outreach, Discipleship, Missions/Ministry and Fellowship Leaders have plans in place to achieve the class' goals in these areas.

- Encourage members to discover their spiritual gifts and to employ them in the various ministries of the church.

- Oversee all class activities. The Shepherd is responsible for what goes on inside and outside the classroom.

- Have at least one event outside the church quarterly.

- **Teach God's word.**

- *Be prepared.* Shepherds are expected to come to class prepared. In 2 Timothy 2:15 we are admonished to "study to shew thyself approved unto God, a workman that needeth not to be ashamed, rightly dividing the word of truth." It is not acceptable for a Shepherd to start preparing for the lesson on the Saturday night before Sunday's class. Dr. McCalep puts it this way: "At the Forest, we do not condone Saturday night specials as preparation for Fulfillment Hour." ***On Sunday evening, the Shepherd should start preparing for the following Sunday's lesson.*** Preparation begins with communing with God, asking God's blessings that His will be done in the classroom.

— *Be theologically sound and rooted in doctrine.* Use the Bible as your textbook. The Sunday School book is only a reference.

— *Be on time.* Fulfillment Hour begins when the first person enters the room. That first person should be the Shepherd. When the first learner arrives, the Shepherd is more than ready to begin sharing what God has placed on his/her heart. You do not need a quota present to begin Fulfillment Hour. Matthew 18:20 says, "For where two or three are gathered together in my name, there am I in the midst of them."

— *Involve the learners.* Allow the principles of God's Word to come alive in the interaction between the Shepherd and the learners. Always have something for the learners to say, see and do. You could say that this also is true in the traditional Sunday School. The teacher sees everybody. Everyone hears what the teacher says and everyone watches whatever the teacher does. Notice that in Fulfillment Hour, the focus is on the learner. The *learner* has something to see. The *learner* has something to say. The *learner* has something to do. This does not mean (as in many traditional Sunday Schools) that the learner would read a verse or couple of verses from the lesson, and then explain what he just read.

— *Lead the learning process.* The Shepherds are expected to lead the class. The class does not lead the Shepherd. Leading the class does not mean lecturing to the class, nor does it mean preaching to the class. Fulfillment Hour learners are expected to take an active role in the Fulfillment Hour class. There is a description for each Fulfillment Hour position in the class (see Appendix 3). There is even a position description for the member. It is not enough to have someone to just come to class. As Bruce Wilkinson states in *Seven Laws of the Learner*, "A teacher is not teaching if the learner is not learning."

— *Listen to the comments made by the class members.* Their words will reveal their level of understanding, degree of growth and areas of need.

- **Minister to the personal needs of the class members.**

  — Encourage the Care Group Leaders to contact their members weekly, and then contact the Care Group Leaders to find out what needs require attention.

— Conduct an annual "Needs Assessment" to determine the spiritual growth needs of the class.

- **Grow more Fulfillment Hour leaders.**
  — Seek out new workers for Fulfillment Hour. Pray for discernment.
  — Lead the class to "twin" (duplicate) itself.
  — Model what it means to be a devoted follower of Christ.
  — Pray regularly, especially for the unit/class members.
  — Read the Bible daily.
  — Know how to share salvation with an unsaved person. Actively seek to lead any unsaved person in the unit/class to accept Jesus Christ as Lord and Savior.
  — Be an example of Christian living and stewardship to the unit/class.
  — Continuously grow in her personal relationship with God.
  — Worship and tithe regularly.
  — Regularly attend Bible Study and/or discipleship training outside of Fulfillment Hour.

- **Strive to be a better Shepherd through ongoing personal development.**
  — Attend all training sessions.

– Attend all Weekly Workers' Meetings.

– Read at least two books related to the work of the Sunday School each year.

- **Fulfill administrative duties.**

    – Maintain an updated class roll, in addition to the Fulfillment Hour Secretary's roll. The Class Secretary helps the Shepherd maintain the roll for the individual Fulfillment Hour class while the Fulfillment Hour Secretary keeps the official composite enrollment for all classes.

    – Support the Fulfillment Hour Coordinator/Director by providing all requested information in a timely manner.

    – Keep an updated class organization chart on file with the Fulfillment Hour Secretary.

The Shepherd's Gifts

The spiritual gifts that enable a Shepherd to effectively fulfill this role are:

- Shepherding (Eph. 4:11-12, 1 Peter 5:1-4, John 10:1-18)
- Leadership (Rom. 12:8, Heb. 13:17, Luke 22:25-26)
- Encouragement (Rom. 12:8, Acts 11:22-24, Acts 15:30-32)
- Evangelism (Eph. 4:11, Acts 8:26-40, Luke 19:1-10)

Notice that "teaching" is not on the list. While the gift of teaching is useful to the Shepherd, we feel that the gifts listed here are more necessary to have the desired influence in the lives of others.

Characteristics of a Good Shepherd

"Good Shepherds" who care for their sheep will:

- Know the characteristics of the class level they are teaching.
- Know each student by name and face and will encourage class members to know each other.
- Know if a guest came into their classes.
- Know personal information about each member and will allow members to know personal information about them.
- Provide support when personal tragedy strikes the lives of their members.
- Know if all of their members are Christians and their spiritual levels.
- Assess the spiritual needs of their class annually.
- Know what influences are affecting their class members.
- Know the desires of their class members.
- Know the ministries in which members of their class are serving.

We believe that the highest calling for a layperson is to be a Shepherd. To be a Fulfillment Hour Shepherd is an opportunity to shape, direct and mold the lives of others. It is by far one of the most exciting and challenging ministry experiences. Being a Shepherd in Fulfillment Hour is the most important thing one can do and it is to be done well. The Shepherd is a biblical leader and must be an example. While the role carries awesome responsibilities, the Shepherd is a Christian and, like Paul, can do all things through Christ which strengtheneth him (Philippians 4:13). Each Fulfillment Hour Shepherd signs an annual commitment to serve in the position for one year.

> *We believe that the highest calling for a layperson is to be a Shepherd. To be a Fulfillment Hour Shepherd is an opportunity to shape, direct and mold the lives of others.*

THE GREATEST OF THESE

(Author Unknown)

Though I have all the Elmer's glue and scissors,
And have read the lesson five times,
And have not love, I am not a Shepherd.

And though I have all the construction paper, glitter and Bible
Posters, puzzles, and unit activities,
And have been in special planning sessions,
And have not love, I am not a Shepherd.
For being a Shepherd is more than being on time,
Present, Bible brought, and lesson prepared.
It's even more than faithfully attending the church services.
A Shepherd looks neat and is not easily provoked
When something is wrong with the heating or cooling system.

A Shepherd is not envious;
Wants not for his/her name to be praised,
But works for the glory of God.
They bear the problems, believe and
Hope for the best for all the children they care for;
For a Shepherd's work is in vain unless he/she
Has true interest in the children.

Where there be magic markers...they shall dry up.
Where there be chalk and blackboards...they shall crumble.
Where there be printed literature...it shall fade.
But a right relationship to God will endure forever
As it is shared in the lives of your students.
All work is a result of His love.

And now abideth planning, preparation and love...
These three... but the greatest of these is love.
For without God's love, all work is naught.

Friendly Reminders for the Fulfillment Hour Shepherd

(1) **DON'T** arbitrarily call on class members to read before the class; **INSTEAD**, ask for volunteers to read when necessary.

(2) **DON'T** stand when teaching children; **INSTEAD**, sit so that you will be physically closer to their eye level.

(3) **DON'T** call on learners to read a verse and then explain what they read; **INSTEAD**, teach them what it means.

(4) **DON'T** embarrass learners when they may answer a question incorrectly; **INSTEAD**, *show* them what the Bible has to say about the issue.

(5) **DON'T** alienate members and/or guests in your class; **INSTEAD**, make everyone feel welcome and glad they came.

(6) **DON'T** insult learners' intelligence by implying only you know the answers; **INSTEAD**, encourage learners to take a meaningful part in the discussion.

(7) **DON'T** act one way and teach another; **INSTEAD**, practice what you teach.

(8) **DON'T** imply that your way is the "only" way; **INSTEAD**, encourage, enlist and involve class members in leadership roles.

(9) **DON'T** keep the class discussion focused on biblical times only; **INSTEAD**, discuss how biblical times relate to what is happening today.

(10) **DON'T** let your class think that your role in their lives has only to do with Fulfillment Hour; **INSTEAD**, make sure your class members know that you are interested in their whole lives.

(11) **DON'T** be overly concerned about the number of members in your class; **INSTEAD**, teach the Word to the members who are present and trust the Holy Spirit to lead you in finding the increase.

(12) **DON'T** wait until "High Attendance Day" to invite others to your class; **INSTEAD**, make every Sunday "High Attendance Day." Invite family, friends and other prospects.

(13) **DON'T** use a lecture-format with preschoolers and children; **INSTEAD**, vary your teaching style. Always have something to DO, something to SEE and something to SAY in every class. Use the resource activities that come with your curriculum materials.

(14) **DON'T** stand before your class holding only your Sunday School book; **INSTEAD**, teach from the Bible. The Sunday School book is only a reference; the Bible is the Fulfillment Hour textbook.

(15) **DON'T** use the word "split" when referring to twinning (duplicating) your class; **INSTEAD**, say, "We are creating a new class to reach new people for Christ."

(16) **DON'T** convene your class off-campus on Sunday morning; **INSTEAD**, meet in the regular class location and at the regular time every Sunday. You never want people to come and not be able to find your class.

(17) **DON'T** cancel your class when you cannot be there; **INSTEAD**, arrange for a substitute Shepherd. If necessary, contact the Fulfillment Hour Administration to help you find someone to teach your class in your absence.

(18) **DON'T** combine your class with another class because you have only a few members; **INSTEAD**, provide ministry touches to the enrollment you already have. Ministry touches are contacts to members and prospects via telephone calls, e-mail, visits, letters and cards. Be constantly contact conscious. Ask people, "Will you be in Fulfillment Hour?"

(19) **DON'T** remove (or request to remove) names from your class roster because of non-attendance; **INSTEAD**, use your class roster as a ministry tool, an opportunity to reach out and care for others, especially those not attending class.

(20) **DON'T** use the entire class period for teaching; **INSTEAD**, allow for community time and the sharing of reports from the ministry position leaders.

(21) **DON'T** wait until Saturday night or Sunday morning to begin studying the Fulfillment Hour lesson; INSTEAD, begin preparing for the next Sunday's lesson immediately following the current lesson.

FULFILLING GOD'S PURPOSES FOR THE CHURCH THROUGH EVANGELISM

"For the Son of man is come to seek and to save that which was lost."—Luke 19:10

Evangelism is the first focus of Fulfillment Hour. The purpose of evangelism is to seek and save the lost. This is done in Fulfillment Hour through evangelistic teaching and witnessing while fulfilling the other purposes of the church—ministry, missions, discipleship and fellowship.

The Fulfillment Hour is the delivery system for the church's Evangelism Ministry. The Pastor or Minister of Evangelism should work closely with the Fulfillment Hour "to equip the body of Christ with practical tools for effectively bringing lost persons to Christ, thus fulfilling the primary purpose of the church." Rev. David Hopewell, Sr., Minister of Evangelism at Greenforest, puts it this way: "God has given all of us a ministry of reconciliation. We are to be ambassadors of Christ and speak His message of salvation to the lost wherever we come in contact with them."

The Evangelism/Outreach Leader's Role

Every adult and youth Fulfillment Hour class is expected to have an Evangelism/Outreach Leader. If a class does not have an Evangelism/Outreach Leader, the Shepherd is (by default) the Evangelism/Outreach Leader for his class. In the Children's and Preschool Divisions, the Shepherd or another adult worker serves as the Evangelism/Outreach Leader for the Fulfillment Hour unit. The Evangelism/Outreach Leader's responsibilities include:

> *Every adult and youth Fulfillment Hour class is expected to have an Evangelism/Outreach Leader. If a class does not have an Evangelism/Outreach Leader, the Shepherd is (by default) the Evangelism/Outreach Leader for his class.*

- Working with the Minister of Evangelism to develop and implement class evangelism, visitation and outreach goals.
- Planning and coordinating outreach/visitation activities for the class.
- Encouraging class members in their personal witnessing.

The Evangelism/Outreach Leader's Duties

The specific tasks or duties associated with the above responsibilities are:

- Lead the class in participating in all evangelism activities.

- Encourage and support class members in developing their personal witnessing styles so that they are comfortable sharing Christ with non-believers.
- Lead the class in participating in weekly visitation of prospects and members.
- Lead the class in inviting people to Fulfillment Hour, i.e., making weekly contacts.
- Assist the class' Discipleship Leader in encouraging the class to participate in evangelism training.
- Participate in the Fulfillment Hour Weekly Workers' Meetings.

The Evangelism/Outreach Leader's Gifts

The Evangelism/Outreach Leader should have a passion for saving the lost and the spiritual gift of evangelism. The Evangelism/Outreach Leader will employ these gifts:

- Evangelism (Eph. 4:11, Acts 8:26-40, Luke 19:1-10)
- Faith (1 Cor. 12:9, 13:2, Heb. 11:1, Rom. 4:18-21)
- Discernment (1 Cor. 12:10, Acts 5:1-4, Matt. 16:21-23)

In any given congregation, a certain percentage of the membership will have a burden for lost people and the gift(s) needed for the work of evangelism. These persons should be intentionally sought to fulfill the positions of Evangelism/Outreach Leader in the Fulfillment Hour classes.

Teaching Evangelistically

Evangelism is sharing the death, burial and resurrection of Jesus for the purpose of leading others to commit their lives to Him. Fulfillment Hour Shepherds are admonished to "teach evangelistically," i.e., teach to save. This means that the plan of salvation should be shared each time the class meets. As a result

> *If everyone in our Fulfillment Hour class is a Christian, we are not really doing our job of reaching the lost.*

of our Fulfillment Hour strategy of fishing (reaching out) with a large net, we have to be prepared to share God's Word with everyone we reach. If everyone in our Fulfillment Hour class is a Christian, we are not really doing our job of reaching the lost.

However, Fulfillment Hour is not limited to success. Although we share the Gospel, it may be another time, another place and other circumstances before an individual actually receives salvation. The focus is not on how many we bring in, but on our obedience to God's command to share the Good News. We merely plant the seed. God provides the increase. "I planted the seed, Apollos watered it, but God made it grow. So neither he who plants nor he who waters is anything, but only God, who makes things grow." (1 Cor. 3:6-7 NIV). It is important that we do not take any credit for the harvest. Instead, we give God the glory for everything we do.

Evangelism through Ministry/Missions, Discipleship and Fellowship

Ministry/missions, discipleship and Fellowship offer tremendous evangelism opportunities.

Ministry/Missions

As the Fulfillment Hour class members minister to the needs of other people within the church, they have the opportunity to share Christ. We never assume that just because someone is a member of the church that he/she is saved. We are always looking for opportunities to offer salvation or provide assurance for those who may have backslid. Likewise, we have opportunities to offer salvation or the assurance of salvation when we minister to people who are outside of our local church.

Discipleship

People come to really know Christ through discipleship training. As their knowledge increases, so does their personal walk with Him. While discipleship training is designed for those who have already accepted Christ, we have found that those who are seeking Him often find their way to accepting Him as their personal savior through discipleship training. That is why we encourage you to open all discipleship training to anyone. Membership in your local church should not be a requirement to attend discipleship training.

Fellowship

Fellowship activities are another way to evangelize. Everyone is invited—class members, family, friends and prospects. Rarely will everyone who is present be saved. It is a wonderful opportunity to show that Christians can have fun and be loving and supportive of one another. We should never let a fellowship event end without offering Christ.

Evangelism opportunities are always present. Our mission is to seek and to save the lost. We must remember that the lost are inside the church as well as outside.

The Joshua Ministry

Greenforest's Fulfillment Hour uses an evangelism strategy called "The Joshua Ministry." This ministry was birthed through the vision of Greenforest's Minister of Evangelism, Rev. David Hopewell, Sr. In Joshua 1:14-15, Joshua repeated Moses' words to the tribes of Reuben, Gad and Manasseh:

"The Lord your God has given you this land. Your wives and your little ones and your cattle, shall remain on this side of the Jordan; but you shall pass before your brothers armed, all the mighty men of valor, and help them; until the Lord has given your brothers rest, as he hath given unto you, and they also have possessed their land which the Lord your God hath given them: then shall you return unto your possession, and enjoy it, which Moses the Lord's servant gave you on this side of the Jordan toward the sunrising."

Joshua explained to the people that they were to leave their own families and possessions to go help their brothers possess their land. They were also to stay there until their brothers were able to handle things on their own. This evangelism approach teaches the Fulfillment Hour classes that as they become blessed with God's Word, they are to leave their comfort zone and go share their blessings of God's love with others who do not know Him. Like Joshua and the tribes, Evangelism/Outreach Leaders are to leave their Fulfillment Hour classes and individual families to go out into the streets with the unbelievers. They should be committed to helping each other in the community.

> *This evangelism approach teaches the Fulfillment Hour classes that as they become blessed with God's Word, they are to leave their comfort zone and go share their blessings of God's love with others who do not know Him.*

The adult Fulfillment Hour classes are divided into the tribes of Israel. (See Appendix 12.) The actual number of tribes depends upon the size of the Fulfillment Hour. At Greenforest, we have the tribes of Ephraim, Gad, Reuben and Manasseh with 20–25 classes assigned to each. Each tribe has a Tribal Leader who is selected and trained by the Pastor or Minister of Evangelism.

Each adult Fulfillment Hour class is expected to go witnessing door-to-door with its tribe for two hours on two Saturdays per month. We call these door-to-door campaigns Evangelism Blitzes. Each blitz targets a specific neighborhood that is pre-selected by the Evangelism Ministry. Before evangelizing a community, the first task is to "spy the land" (Josh. 2:1). It is important to get a sense of the people who live in the community and their needs. Fulfillment Hour class members are encouraged to invite tribes to evangelize in their neighborhoods.

As with other ministry activities, indepth evangelism training is provided before anyone goes into the community on an Evangelism Blitz. The Evangelism Minister or a trained Tribal Leader presents this training in a "Soul-Winning Workshop." The training usually takes one and a half hours and is immediately followed by a blitz. The workshop includes:

- Biblical Reasons for Why We Should Witness
- Overcoming Fear and Anxiety
- How to Share Your Testimony
- Role Play
- Questions and Answers

The workshop teaches believers to allow the Holy Spirit to lead them in personal evangelism. They are taught that they need to be prepared for spiritual battle and dressed in the whole armor of God as they go forward to meet the tasks before them. By the end of the workshop, the participants have the ability and comfort to knock on doors.

The workshop participants are divided into teams at the end of the training. Each team is assigned specific house numbers or streets for the neighborhood. The teams are given literature that tells the Gospel (tracts) and brochures with information about the church. Each team designates a recorder to record the action taken and results at

> *The goal of each Fulfillment Hour class is to evangelize and meet the needs of those living in their class members' neighborhoods.*

each home that is visited. The teams are instructed to return to the classroom at a specific time. Before going out, the ministry's activities are bathed in prayer. Intercessory prayer is given for all participants and all potential receivers of God's salvation. God is asked to bless all of the ministry's activities. At the end of the blitz, the tribe returns to the church and each team reports on their activities. God is given all the praise for every good thing that happens.

The Evangelism/Outreach Leaders are taught that sharing the Good News is not a one-time deal, but a *continuous campaign*. The goal of each Fulfillment Hour class is to evangelize and meet the needs of those living in the neighborhoods of their class members. The Evangelism tribe knocks on doors, shares the Gospel, and tries to meet as many needs as possible. Every evanglism encounter includes prayer for the individual and his family. After completing these efforts in a neighborhood, the tribe moves on to help other members possess their land.

The Kingdom of God is built on relationships. Since the most effective way to evangelize is through relationships, each Evangelism tribe builds relationships by meeting needs and becoming involved in the lives of those they encounter. Once a person's need is prayed for and a relationship bond begins, the door for sharing the Gospel is opened a little wider.

There are four phases to the Joshua Ministry:

Phase I. "Members Helping Members"

Members of Fulfillment Hour classes volunteer their own neighborhoods for the location of the Evangelism Blitzes.

Phase II. "Churches Helping Churches"

Neighborhood churches join together to evangelize in their communities.

Phase III. "Joshua Generation: God's Witnessing Army"

The Joshua Generation consists of young adults and teens. This army fulfills a specific need. In many instances, young people don't want to hear from adults. They consider any adult to be "the outsider, the establishment, the enemy." However, talking to their peers can make a gigantic difference to some. The Joshua Generation has their own training sessions designed for their age group.

Phase IV. Special Forces Team

The Special Forces Team is a group of believers who go that added mile to share God's Word. The Special Forces Team assists churches in planting and engaging in nighttime evangelism. You might see the Special Forces Team out on New Year's Eve night, on Halloween night, in the streets, on the corners, in the malls, in the bars or in the nightclub—anywhere there is an opportunity to share God's Word to a lost soul.

Darrell Robinson says in *People Sharing Jesus* that we ***must share Jesus with confidence and in a non-threatening way.*** You share Jesus with people by meeting them where they are. They are on one of eight levels:

- Ignorance
- Indifference
- Hostility
- Interest
- Conviction
- Conversion

- Growing
- Spiritually Declining

The Joshua Ministry is about helping our brothers possess all that God intended for them and discipling them until they

> The Joshua Ministry is about helping our brothers possess all that God intended for them and discipling them until they are able to take care of themselves

are able to take care of themselves. Our help begins with meeting people and their needs where they are. To learn more about the Joshua Ministry, read *The Joshua Ministry: God's Witnessing Army* by Rev. David Hopewell, Sr.

In summary, seeking and saving the lost is the primary purpose of the church and, therefore, the primary focus of Fulfillment Hour. By using the strategies of evangelistic teaching, the Joshua Ministry, ministry/missions, discipleship, and fellowship, the Fulfillment Hour effectively fulfills the purposes of God through evangelism.

FULFILLING GOD'S PURPOSES FOR THE CHURCH THROUGH DISCIPLESHIP

"Go ye therefore, and teach all nations, baptizing them in the name of the Father, and of the Son, and of the Holy Ghost."
—Matt. 28:19, 20

In the Great Commission (Matt. 28:19-20), Jesus told us to "make disciples." One of the five purposes of the church is to "make disciples." The purpose of the church's Discipleship Ministry is ***"to teach the people of God to obey the commands of God."*** The Pastor, Minister of Discipleship or Minister/Director of Christian Education typically leads the Discipleship Ministry. The goal is to provide continuous training and opportunities for spiritual growth outside of Fulfillment Hour. The training should include weekly Bible study and periodic discipleship workshops. ***Fulfillment Hour supports the church's Discipleship Ministry by encouraging class members to regularly attend Bible Study and discipleship training opportunities.***

The Discipleship Leader's Role

Each adult and youth class is asked to select at least one Discipleship Leader. At Greenforest, we have male and female Discipleship Leaders for each adult class. This facilitates gender-specific study groups (more about that later). If a class does not have a Discipleship Leader, then the Shepherd is the Discipleship Leader by default. The Shepherd is the Discipleship Leader in all Children's and Preschool Fulfillment Hour units.

The Fulfillment Hour Discipleship Leader is responsible for:

- Involving class members in the church's Discipleship Ministry.
- Encouraging class members to grow spiritually through individual and/or small group study.
- Encouraging members to discover and employ their spiritual gifts in the work of the church.

The Discipleship Leader's Duties

The specific tasks the Discipleship Leader performs are:

- Work with the Shepherd to assess the class' spiritual growth needs annually.
- Work with the Minister of Discipleship to develop and implement Discipleship training goals for the class.

- Stay informed of all training that is offered by the Discipleship Ministry.
- Keep all class members aware of the need and opportunities for discipleship training.
- Encourage class members to attend Bible Study regularly.
- Encourage class members to take discipleship training workshops individually and/or as a group.
- Encourage members to take spiritual gifts training and to put their gifts to work in the ministries of the church.
- Lead and/or coordinate small group study sessions outside of Fulfillment Hour.
- Assist the Shepherd and the Minister of Discipleship in providing training opportunities for class members.
- Lead class members in witnessing and making other disciples.
- Encourage members in their daily Christian walk.
- Be disciplined in his/her personal prayer, Bible study and devotional life.
- Constantly seek to mature in his/her relationship with God and be transformed into the likeness of Christ.
- Participate in the Fulfillment Hour Weekly Workers' Meetings.

The Discipleship Leader's Gifts

The Discipleship Leader should have a passion for teaching others to live Christ-like lives. The spiritual gifts that the Discipleship Leader will most often employ are:

- Teaching (Rom. 12:7, 1 Cor. 12:28-29, Acts 18:24-28)
- Encouragement (Rom. 12:8, Acts 11:22-24, Acts 15:30-32)
- Administration (1 Cor. 12:28, Acts 6:1-7, Ex. 18:13-26)

Setting Discipleship Goals

The Fulfillment Hour Discipleship Leader encourages the class to set discipleship goals either individually or as a group over a given period of time, usually a year. The discipleship goal is the number of courses that the class takes outside of Fulfillment Hour.

> *The Fulfillment Hour Discipleship Leader encourages the class to set discipleship goals...*

The Discipleship Leader maintains a written record of the courses taken by the class, and periodically reports to the class its status in reaching or surpassing their goal. Recognition should be given to classes that meet and/or exceed their goals.

Individual Study

All class members, including the Shepherd, should participate in regular Bible study. Bible study obviously takes place in Fulfillment Hour. However, the Discipleship Leader is to encourage everyone to have a personal Bible study program that goes beyond Fulfillment Hour. Personal Bible study is essential to spiritual maturity.

The Fulfillment Hour Discipleship Leader also encourages class members to take the Bible study courses and workshops offered by the church's Discipleship Ministry. Through Bible study and discipleship training, Fulfillment Hour members learn:

> *The Fulfillment Hour Discipleship Leader also encourages class members to take the Bible study courses and workshops offered by the church's Discipleship Ministry.*

- Who God is.
- Who they are in relationship to Him.
- How to love God.
- How much God loves them.
- How the Holy Spirit works within believers.
- How to study His Word.
- How to obey His commands.
- How to live a life of faith.

Small Group Study

The purpose of small group study is to join together a group of believers who want to grow spiritually and become better disciples of Christ so they can make other disciples. The groups determine what they study and how often they meet. The only requirement is that they do not meet during

Fulfillment Hour or worship services. They can meet at the church or in members' homes.

As in everything, the first step in creating a study group is prayer. You must pray for God's guidance in whatever you do. Pray for courage and for God to lead you. Ask God to help you discern your group's needs. Then ask Him to speak to those needs. One way of assessing needs is by simply asking the group. You can formalize the assessment by using a questionnaire that asks members to list and prioritize the areas in which they need to grow.

Once you have determined the study topic(s), ask for volunteers in your class to sign-up for your study group. The study group can be comprised of two to ten participants. The Discipleship Leader does not have to lead every study session. The Discipleship Leader is responsible for making sure the study groups are available. In fact, a good way to grow more Discipleship Leaders is by asking other class members to share their gifts and knowledge by leading these small group study sessions. Also, you can invite ministers or laypeople with expertise in the subject matter to lead the group.

If you will be leading the group, you must prepare ahead of time. Preparation should be doused in prayer. Pray for God to give you the message He knows your group needs. Pray for the participants. Pray that God will be glorified in all that is done in your study group. Then prepare an outline with a list of key points and discussion questions. During the session, encourage everyone to participate. Allow the Holy Spirit to guide you throughout the entire session. Always close the session in prayer, remembering to give God praise for all results. Be sure to inform the Fulfillment Hour Administration of your group's activities.

At Greenforest, we have taken the small study groups a step further by charging the male and female Discipleship Leaders to lead separate men's and women's groups in the study of the book, *Growing Up to the Head: 10 Essentials to Becoming a Better Christian,* by our Pastor, Dr. George O. McCalep, Jr. *Growing Up to the Head* presents principles for growing the church numerically through individual spiritual growth. The book is the cornerstone of discipleship at Greenforest. Having separate men's and women's groups allows class members to candidly discuss issues that they may not feel comfortable addressing when members of the opposite sex are present. Monthly "Train-the-Trainer" classes are held for the Discipleship Leaders who facilitate these study groups.

Discipleship at Greenforest

The following describes the ongoing discipleship training at Greenforest. We share this as an example of what can be done when an effective Discipleship Ministry is in place. Our Minister of Discipleship oversees all discipleship training activities. Greenforest's Discipleship Ministry consists of the following elements:

- Wednesday Night Bible Study
- The Track Around the Forest
- Saturday Hol(y)istic School
- Spiritual Gifts Ministry

The following describes each of the elements of our Discipleship Ministry.

Wednesday Night Bible Study

Greenforest offers Bible Study classes every Wednesday night for all ages—adult, youth, children and preschool. The classes provide small group studies of various books and themes in the Bible. The teacher usually selects the topic based on the needs of the class. Thus, each class studies a different topic, except in January when the Pastor selects a specific book of the Bible that everyone focuses on for one month. The book is selected according to the direction in which the Holy Spirit is leading the church.

Track Around the Forest

The Greenforest Discipleship Training Institute is called "Track Around the Forest." The concept is drawn from an athletic track with four lanes. Each lane contains progressive discipleship courses. Members are asked to run a lap each year, that is, complete a series of related courses in the same lane.

The "Track Around the Forest" course schedule is published annually and includes the course number, course title, textbook, textbook price, instructor, room location, training dates, and length of training (in weeks) listed by quarter. The courses are offered on Wednesday nights in addition to Wednesday Night Bible Study.

Saturday Hol(y)istic School

On Saturdays, our Discipleship Ministry presents Hol(y)istic classes. These classes include training that benefits the total person (spiritually, mentally, emotionally and physically). Hol(y)istic classes include home buying seminars, computer classes, sign language, crocheting, aerobics, etc.

Spiritual Gifts Ministry

The Spiritual Gifts Ministry is a way of doing church that complements the Fulfillment Hour Model. Ultimately, the aim of the Spiritual Gifts Ministry is to have every member of the church identify and develop his/her spiritual gifts as well as have them matched and fully utilized in one of the many ministries of the church.

Our Spiritual Gifts Ministry offers an eight-week class to help members discern their gifts, the area of ministry to which they are called and the tasks they have been called to perform. At the end of the class, they are matched to an existing ministry or given guidance on how to start a new ministry. Through this process, the Spiritual Gifts Ministry is a resource pool for recruiting Fulfillment Hour workers. The Fulfillment Hour Discipleship Leader encourages all members to attend Spiritual Gifts training so they can discern their gifts and become actively involved in the ministries of the church.

Characteristics of Disciples

Dr. McCalep shares in his book, *Sin in the House*, that "a disciple is a disciplined learner and devoted follower who is willing to make another disciple." He also states that "discipleship involves growing up in the likeness of Christ." Being a disciple of Jesus means:

> "A disciple is a disciplined learner and devoted follower who is willing to make another disciple."

(1) **Following His teachings.** "Even as he spoke, many put their faith in Him. To the Jews who had believed him, Jesus said, 'If you hold to my teaching, you are really my disciples. Then you will know the truth, and the truth will set you free.' " (John 8:30-32 NIV)

(2) **Self-denial.** "But when Jesus turned and looked at his disciples, he rebuked Peter. 'Get behind me, Satan!' He said. 'You do not have in mind the things of God, but the things

of men.' Then He called the crowd to Him along with His disciples and said: 'If anyone would come after me, he must deny himself and take up his cross and follow me. For whoever wants to save his life will lose it, but whoever loses his life for me and for the gospel will save it.' " (Mark 8:33-35 NIV)

(3) Regularly praying to the Father. "One day Jesus was praying in a certain place. When he finished, one of his disciples said to him, Lord, teach us to pray, just as John taught his disciples. He said to them, when you pray, say: Father, hallowed be your name, your kingdom come." (Luke 11:1-2 NIV)

(4) Living day-by-day through faith. This faith is rewarded by eternal life in Jesus Christ. "Then Jesus told him, 'Because you have seen me, you have believed; blessed are those who have not seen and yet have believed.' Jesus did many other miraculous signs in the presence of His disciples, which are not recorded in this book. But these are written that you may believe that Jesus is the Christ, the Son of God, and that by believing you may have life in his name." (John 20:29-31 NIV)

(5) Speaking out against another's ungodly wishes. "Blessed is the king who comes in the name of the Lord! Peace in heaven and glory in the highest! Some of the

Pharisees in the crowd said to Jesus, 'Teacher, rebuke your disciples!' 'I tell you,' He replied, 'if they keep quiet, the stones will cry out.'" (Luke 19:38-40 NIV)

Being a disciple is certainly not easy, but it is the responsibility of every Christian. For the Fulfillment Hour Discipleship Leader, it is more than personal growth, it is a matter of making other disciples. That is how Fulfillment Hour fulfills the purposes of God through discipleship.

FULFILLING GOD'S PURPOSES FOR THE CHURCH THROUGH FELLOWSHIP

"And they continued steadfastly in the apostles' doctrine and fellowship, and in breaking of bread, and in prayers."—Acts 2:42

Fulfillment Hour uses John 13:34-35 as its springboard Scripture in developing the fellowship function. It states: "A new commandment I give unto you. That ye love one another; as I have loved you, that ye also love one another. By this shall all men know that ye are my disciples, if ye have love one to another." The Bible tells us that the early Christians continued in "fellowship" and that they were known by their love for one another.

We are called to fellowship daily with Jesus Christ. "God is faithful, by whom ye were called unto the fellowship of his Son Jesus Christ our Lord" (1 Cor. 1:9). In Corinth, Christians did not have one, central meeting place. There were no church buildings. Christians met in various homes or wherever they could. Even during this time, fellowship was a major part of worship service.

Each Fulfillment Hour class is a family. The Fulfillment Hour family needs to bond one to another, just as you would with your biological family. Fulfillment Hour classes are encouraged to have regular fellowship activities. A fellowship

> The Fulfillment Hour Fellowship Leader plans and coordinates activities that will facilitate good personal relationships within the class.

activity is any informal activity that allows the members to share themselves with each other. The activities may occur during the regular Sunday School hour or outside the class. It is at these fellowships that class members get to really know each other and relationships are nurtured.

The Fellowship Leader's Role

The Fulfillment Hour Fellowship Leader's main responsibility is to assist the Shepherd in building nurturing relationships within the class. To this end, the Fulfillment Hour Fellowship Leader plans and coordinates activities that will facilitate good personal relationships within the class. Developing good personal relationships is an important step in maintaining a great Fulfillment Hour class. The Fellowship Leader's responsibilities include:

- Building caring relationships among the class members
- Assimilating new members into the class
- Developing and implementing class fellowship goals

The Fellowship Leader's Duties

The Fellowship Leader performs the following duties:

- Develops and implements class fellowship goals. A class fellowship goal could be that the class would strive to participate in at least one fellowship activity each month.

- Coordinates fellowship events. This includes class and church-wide fellowship activities. Fellowships could be developed with other classes or other departments. An example would be a fellowship among all of the classes within the Adult Division or a specific department. Don't forget about fellowships with other churches.

- Assimilates new members. The Fellowship Leader makes sure new members are made to feel welcome and helps them become comfortable with the group.

- Attends the Fulfillment Hour Weekly Workers' Meeting.

The Fellowship Leader's Gifts

The spiritual gifts the Fellowship Leader will primarily employ are:

- Hospitality (1 Peter 4:9-10, Rom. 12:13, Heb. 13:1-2)
- Creative Communication (Psalm 150:3-5, 2 Sam. 6:14-15, Mark 4:2, 33)
- Helps (1 Cor. 12:28, Rom. 12:7, Acts 6:1-4, Rom. 16:1-2)

Community Time

During the class period, time should be allotted for the class to get to know each other in a more personal way.

> During the class period, time should be allotted for the class to get to know each other in a more personal way.

Community time is a time for building relationships. It does not have to take significant time away from regular class activities. To the contrary, it can last only five to eight minutes. Here's an example of a class community time activity:

First, the Fellowship Leader must be present and on time. The Fellowship Leader stands at the door and greets each member, handing him a written number—1, 2, 3 or 4. All persons with like numbers assemble into a group. There should be four groups. The leader gives the groups four minutes to find out four things they have in common that are *not church-related*. After the four minutes are up, each group is given one minute to report what they learned. After each report, the Fellowship Leader praises the group. This is a fun, fast way to build relationships as the members get to know each other.

Open Invitation

Every member in the Fulfillment Hour class should be invited to every fellowship. Every member should also make a habit of inviting prospects to each fellowship. Family members of the Fulfillment Hour class members should be welcome to the fellowship. For example, if a husband is a member of the Men's Bible Class and the wife is a member of the Women's Bible Class, when either class is having a fellowship, the spouse should feel welcome to come and participate. ***A Fulfillment Hour fellowship is not a closed fellowship.***

> *Every member in the Fulfillment Hour class should be invited to every fellowship.*

Fellowship activities provide the opportunity for class members to get to know each other as friends. As the class relationships grow, the friendships grow. As our friendships and relationships with one another grow, our friendship and relationship with God grows. Fulfillment Hour fosters the belief that classes bond together in Christ.

Planning Successful Fellowship Activities

A fellowship activity, as with all other activities, should meet the following requirements for approval:

(1) Fulfill one or more of the purposes of the church.

(2) Fall in line with the overall mission of the church.

(3) Remain within the allotted line item budget.

(4) Remain within the allotted time.

(5) Result in giving God all the praise.

Follow these steps to have a successful fellowship activity:

Step 1: Select the type of event.

Each fellowship activity should have a purpose that fulfills a task of Fulfillment Hour. Involve the whole class. Get their suggestions or recommendations. Encourage the class to be creative in planning fellowships. (See Appendix 13 for sample activities.) It does not have to be a party, nor does it have to be centered on a holiday. Knowing that you will never be able to please 100% of the people, select an activity that will appeal to the majority of the class. *(Note: In children's or preschool classes/units, the Shepherds and other adult workers should perform the planning of the activity.)*

> *Each fellowship activity should have a purpose that fulfills a task of Fulfillment Hour.*

Step 2: Select a date.

Check the church's calendar to make sure there is no conflict with a previously scheduled church activity. Several dates should be initially selected, along with varying times. This will give you some flexibility in case there is a conflicting event on your first choice of dates.

Step 3: Select a location.

A fellowship that is held away from the church has a better chance of permitting the class members to open up to one another, resulting in the class getting to know one another better. We have found it best to hold the event at a neutral location. While it is wonderful when members open their homes to the class, it could potentially lead to less participation. People may dread when it is their turn to host because of the work and cost involved. Others may feel uncomfortable if their homes are not as nice.

> A fellowship that is held away from the church has a better chance of permitting the class members to open up to one another, resulting in the class getting to know one another better.

It is always good to have an alternate location in mind in case your first choice is not available.

Step 4: Select the menu.

Next, select the food you want to serve. List the food and other items needed for the fellowship, and distribute the list among the class so that class members can volunteer to bring specific items. (See Appendix 14.) Be careful not to over-emphasize the food requirement or expectation. You do not want to discourage anyone from participating. This is important because you want to get the entire class involved in the activity.

Step 5: Plan your activities.

Fellowship activities should be thought out thoroughly before being implemented. Each fellowship should be viewed as a ministry opportunity to bring others closer to Jesus Christ.

When you plan activities for children and preschool participants, remember that the children cannot drive themselves.

> When planning adult events, plan activities for their children.

An adult has to take them to the planned events. Therefore, be sure to involve parents when planning activities for children and preschool Fulfillment Hour classes.

When planning adult events, plan activities for their children. Have something fun for all ages that will be present. Look for opportunities for the children to participate with the adults. This is a great way to teach the children how they can have fun in a Christian environment.

Step 6: Estimate your budget.

An itemized budget for each activity, as well as budget justification, should be given to the Shepherd if the church will need to bear some of the expense for the event. Follow your church's procedures for requesting checks and reimbursements. Be sure to start this process at least a month in advance of the activity.

Fellowship activities should never be a financial burden to anyone. However, each person should be encouraged to participate in some way. This could mean bringing a covered dish, bringing needed supplies or participating in the setup and/or cleanup activities.

Step. 7: Invite everyone.

Invite all class members and prospects. Particularly target the new members and prospects. In the relaxed atmosphere of a fellowship, class members can be transparent and show their true selves. New members and prospects then get a chance to see the members outside of their *church* attire and demeanor. Family members are automatically invited. Adult workers who provide support services to your class should also be invited.

Use invitations, personal phone calls, visits, e-mails, etc. The key is to have individuals R.S.V.P. so you will know the number of people for which you need to plan.

Step 8: Advise the Fulfillment Hour Administration.

A calendar of fellowship activities and an itemized budget should be provided to the Fulfillment Hour Administration by each division. The Shepherd is responsible for ensuring that this information is communicated to the administrative staff.

In conclusion, Fulfillment Hour is built on relationships. Loving relationships can lead non-believers to Christ and believers to spiritual maturity. Loving relationships can also increase

> *It is through loving relationships that Fulfillment Hour fulfills the purposes of God through fellowship.*

involvement in Fulfillment Hour and the work of the church. Finally, loving relationships mean that members will care for each other's needs. It is through loving relationships that Fulfillment Hour fulfills the purposes of God through fellowship.

CHAPTER 10

"Master, which is the great commandment in the law?
Jesus said unto him, Thou shalt love the Lord they God with
all thy heart, and with all thy soul, and with all thy mind.
This is the first and great commandment. And the second is like
unto it, Thou shalt love thy neighbor as thyself."—Matt. 22:36-39

Fulfillment Hour realizes that God expects us to be about His business of helping others. The greatest commandment given to us is this: "Thou shalt love thy God with all thy heart, and with all thy soul, and with all thy mind." (Matt. 22:37) And the second greatest commandment is "Thou shalt love thy neighbor as thyself." (Matt. 22:36-39) As we study the Holy Bible, the Fulfillment Hour textbook, we see that Jesus Christ is our example for ministry and missions. Through example, He taught His disciples how to serve others.

Ministry vs. Missions

In Fulfillment Hour, we recognize that there is a difference between ministry and missions. However, a natural overlap exists between the two because both have to do with assisting others. The dividing point is where the "others" reside. Ministry involves working with people inside the church, whereas missions involve working with people outside the church.

Ministry

Every believer has a spiritual gift. God gives each Christian one or more spiritual gifts to use to minister to the body of Christ. (Eph. 4:11-12) In *The Biblical Basis of Missions,* Avery Willis, Jr. says, "Spiritual gifts are given by God, not chosen by Christians. God determines the gifts you have and the ministry you perform. You are not to covet another's gifts or look down on your own. If you have a particular gift, you have no reason to be proud; or if you do not have a particular gift, you need not be embarrassed. God decides."

> *Ministry involves working with people inside the church, whereas missions involve working with people outside the church.*

Spiritual gifts are manifested in service for the good of other people. There are 23 spiritual gifts. They include teaching, giving, administration, service, prophecy, mercy, wisdom, tongues, evangelism and exhortation. Fulfillment Hour encourages every member, especially every position leader, to discover their spiritual gifts and put them into service. Dr. George McCalep's book entitled *Stir Up the Gifts: Empowering Believers for Victorious Living and Ministry Tasks* is an excellent text about employing spiritual gifts in the work of the church. We believe that every Christian should know his or her gifts and continually be in the process of using them. We also believe that ***although believers may have the same gifts, each believer has a unique purpose and place in the body of Christ. The whole body suffers when believers do not fill their unique purpose.***

> As the church's delivery system, Fulfillment Hour helps to place people in the areas where they have a passion for service so they can use their gifts for the tasks that God has called them to perform.

As the church's delivery system, Fulfillment Hour helps to place people in the areas where they have a passion for service so they can use their gifts for the tasks that God has called them to perform.

Missions

Fulfillment Hour classes are encouraged to participate in domestic and foreign missionary projects. Missions provide Fulfillment Hour another opportunity to mobilize the delivery system in supporting specific projects. Examples of such projects are:

- Food for hurricane and flood victims
- Toiletries for people in disadvantaged countries
- Sunday School books for small churches

The opportunities are infinite for Fulfillment Hour classes to fulfill God's purposes through missions.

Fulfillment Hour classes are also taught to pray for missionaries who are in service spreading the good news of God's love and to encourage them by sending supplies, money, cards, letters and e-mail. Fulfillment Hour members and classes are encouraged to become pen pals with foreign missionaries.

> Fulfillment Hour members and classes are encouraged to become pen pals with foreign missionaries.

Fulfillment Hour leaders with missionary experience are asked to share their experiences to help motivate members to support these programs.

The Ministry/Missions Leaders' Role

Each class is encouraged to have both a Ministry Project Leader and a Missions Leader. These leaders share information with the appropriate church ministry when a class member or prospect needs services that are offered by the church. At the same time, the church's ministries share with the Fulfillment Hour classes various ministry/mission project activities in which classes can provide support. This gives the Fulfillment Hour an opportunity to demonstrate God's love by assisting in crisis intervention that may include food, financial assistance and emergency assistance.

The Ministry/Missions Leaders' Duties

The duties of the Ministry/Missions Leaders are:

- Develop and implement ministry/mission goals for the class.
- Plan and coordinate projects that meet the needs of people within the church.
- Plan and coordinate projects that meet the needs of people outside the church locally, nationally and internationally.
- Lead the class in supporting all ministry/missions projects.
- Lead the class in supporting missionaries through prayer and offerings.
- Identify ways to meet the special needs of members and prospects who are homebound or away from home.
- Participate in the Fulfillment Hour Weekly Workers' Meetings.

The Ministry/Missions Leaders' Gifts

The spiritual gifts that are most commonly employed by Ministry/Missions Leaders are:

- Mercy (Rom. 12:8, Matt. 5:7, Mark 10:46-52)

- Giving (Rom. 12:8, 2 Cor. 6:8, Luke 21:1-4)
- Helps (1 Cor. 12:28, Rom. 12:7, Acts 6:1-4, Rom. 16:1-2)
- Intercession (Rom. 8:26-27, John 17:9-26, 1 Tim. 2:1-2, Col. 1:9-12, 4:12-13)

Care Group Leaders

Care Group Leaders assist the Ministry/Missions Leaders by staying in touch with the class members and finding out their needs. Each Fulfillment Hour class should have at least two Care Group Leaders. The class is divided into groups, each of which has a Care Group Leader. Every class member should be assigned to a Care Group Leader. The Care Group Leader is responsible for ministering to the needs of the learners in his/her group. Consequently, the Fulfillment Hour Care Group Leader

> *The Fulfillment Hour Care Group Leader should contact the members in his or her group on a weekly basis.*

should contact the members in his or her group on a weekly basis. This contact should come in the form of a telephone call, visit, card, letter, e-mail, etc. (See Appendix 3 for the Care Group Leader's ministry position description.)

The Fulfillment Hour class is able to demonstrate compassion through the Care Group Leaders just as Jesus taught the disciples. "Jesus called his disciples to Him and said, 'I have compassion for these people; they have already been with me three days and have nothing to eat. I do not want to send them away hungry, or they may collapse on the way.'" (Matt. 15:32 NIV)

Ministry/Missions at Greenforest

Our Fulfillment Hour works hand-in-hand with the church's Social Ministry. The mission of the Social Ministry is to demonstrate God's love by assisting in one-on-one crisis intervention that may include food, financial assistance and emergency assistance to prevent homelessness. The Social Ministry also provides counseling and social/human/health service referrals in addition to making referrals for financial assistance. This is accomplished by working cooperatively with appropriate agencies and service providers.

The Fulfillment Hour Ministry/Missions Leaders share information with the Social Ministry when someone needs their services. At the same time, the Social Ministry shares with the Fulfillment Hour classes various ministry/mission project activities in which they need help.

The Fulfillment Hour Ministry/Missions Leaders share information with the Social Ministry when someone needs their services. At the same time, the Social Ministry shares with the Fulfillment Hour classes various ministry/mission project activities in which they need help.

Holiday Baskets

One of the mission projects that our Fulfillment Hour actively participates in is the giving of Thanksgiving and Christmas baskets to needy families. Each Fulfillment Hour class tells the Fulfillment Hour Administration how many baskets they would like to give for each holiday. This list is then given to the Social Ministry who assigns needy families to each Fulfillment Hour class equal to the number of baskets committed.

The Social Ministry provides a list of food and other items that should be placed in each basket. Members of the Fulfillment Hour class deliver the baskets to the needy families. The Fulfillment Hour class ministers to the needs of the family in addition to delivering the baskets. Prayer is held with each family and Christ is shared. The families are invited to Fulfillment Hour, worship and Bible Study. It is always made clear that they do not have to be members to participate in anyactivity at Greenforest. In some instances, Fulfillment Hour classes have adopted the family for the entire year.

Deacon Family Ministry

The Greenforest Deacon Family Ministry Plan Resource Book states that "the servant role of the Deacon is also in keeping with Jesus' concern for ministry." The Deacon Family Ministry is an attending/caring approach to ministry that assures that the church remains personal and intimate as it grows. Each member is assigned a Deacon who acts as an assistant to the Pastor on whatever personal issues and concerns that may arise. Ideally, the Deacon Family Ministry has no more than 18–20 families that minister to one another. The Deacon Family Ministry works in conjunction with the Social Ministry to meet the needs of the membership. Fulfillment Hour is an active party to this alliance because in many instances, the Fulfillment Hour Care Group Leaders and Outreach/Evangelism Leaders bring various needs to the attention of the Deacon Family Ministry or the Social Ministry.

> *The Fulfillment Hour Care Group Leaders and Outreach/Evangelism Leaders bring various needs to the attention of the Deacon Family Ministry or the Social Ministry.*

Feed the Homeless

Fulfillment Hour classes also participate in the Feed the Homeless Ministry, which began out of one Fulfillment Hour member's passion for the poor. Every Saturday morning, members from various auxiliaries prepare over 500 lunches to deliver to homeless people in various locations in the metropolitan Atlanta area.

Other Projects

Ministry/mission activities are also implemented in conjunction with other church ministries, e.g., the Prison Ministry, Dialysis Ministry, Alcoholics Anonymous and various support groups. Our Fulfillment Hour classes also supply their own ideas for ministry/mission projects for their classes. The main requirement for a project to be approved for involvement by a Fulfillment Hour class is that the project must have as its goal "to give God all the praise."

Fulfillment Hour helps the church promote self-sufficiency in the community. Self-sufficiency begins with the family. Implementing programs that empower families will ultimately result in freedom from all forms of public dependency. In Fulfillment Hour, we believe that *people don't care how much you know until they know how much you care.* The ministry/mission projects allow individual class members to show that they care. That is how Fulfillment Hour fulfills the purposes of God through ministry/missions.

FULFILLING GOD'S PURPOSES FOR THE CHURCH THROUGH WORSHIP

"Praise ye the Lord. Sing unto the Lord a new song, and his praise in the congregation of saints."—Psalm 149:1

Fulfillment Hour fulfills the purposes of God through worship by teaching and preparing believers to expressively show love and adoration to God, publicly and privately. One of our church's core values states: "We believe that all the primary purposes of the church, except corporate worship, can be fulfilled within the context of a growth-oriented Sunday School." So why can't corporate worship be fulfilled in Fulfillment Hour? Corporate worship is the assembly of the body of believers in a large group setting where the Word of God is preached and God is praised. This does not mean that worship is not a true task of the Fulfillment Hour. To the contrary, worship is very important in the life of every believer and, therefore, is a very important part of Fulfillment Hour. ***In fact, one of the requirements for becoming a Fulfillment Hour Shepherd is that the individual must worship regularly.***

As shown on the Fulfillment Hour Model in the front of the book, Fulfillment Hour is in the center of all we do and are about, rather than worship. That means that all of the other ministries and activities of the church, including worship, flow from the center, the nucleus, which is Fulfillment Hour.

Although corporate worship does not take place during Fulfillment Hour, worship service is a natural outgrowth of Fulfillment Hour. *In Sin in the House*, Dr. George O. McCalep , Jr. shares that "failure to worship, as God through His Word (Scripture) has told us, is a high crime of sin."

As we teach evangelistically in Fulfillment Hour, our underlying foundational strategy is to lead people to faith in the Lord Jesus Christ. In Fulfillment Hour, we all rejoice when a soul is snatched from the hands of the devil. Fulfillment Hour Shepherds are encouraged to walk down the aisle with new converts when they give their lives to the Lord. This creates a connection between what happens in Fulfillment Hour and what happens in worship service.

> *Fulfillment Hour Shepherds are encouraged to walk down the aisle with new converts when they give their lives to the Lord.*

Fulfillment Hour is about leading people to worship. In Fulfillment Hour, we teach that we are to worship God and God only. Exodus 20:4-6 (NIV) states:

"You shall not make for yourself an idol in the form of anything in heaven above or on the earth beneath or in the waters below. You shall not bow down to them or worship them; for I, the Lord your God, am a jealous God, punishing the children for the sin of the fathers to the third and fourth generation of those who hate me, but showing love to a thousand (generations) of those who love me and keep my commandments."

True worship means expressing our adoration, devotion and honor to God because of who He is and our love for Him.

We express our thankfulness when we worship. Though we call a regular church service a time of worship, our lives should be lived as if every moment was a moment of worship. In our Fulfillment Hour classes, we learn how to worship God. Exodus 23:24-26 (NIV) teaches us:

> *In our Fulfillment Hour classes, we learn how to worship God.*

"Do not bow down before their gods or worship them or follow their practices. You must demolish them and break their sacred stones to pieces. Worship the Lord your God, and his blessing will be on your food and water. I will take away sickness from among you, and none will miscarry or be barren in your land. I will give you a full life span."

Some churches may have a Worship and Praise Leader, others may have a Praise Team, yet all depend on congregational participation in the praise period. The specifics do not matter. Fulfillment Hour can contribute to the training of praise participants of any type format. ***Fulfillment Hour learners are taught the importance of and particulars involved in praise.*** We teach that we should praise God for all things, but particularly for His endless, awesome love.

The Prayer Leader's Role

A part of praise is prayer. Each Fulfillment Hour class should have a designated Prayer Leader. If a class does not have a Prayer Leader, the Shepherd by default is the Prayer Leader.

> *Each Fulfillment Hour class should have a designated Prayer Leader.*

The Prayer Leader's main job is to lead the class in public and personal prayer. Each Fulfillment Hour class is encouraged to begin and end everything that is done in prayer. Every activity should be carefully washed in prayer.

When praying publicly, the Prayer Leader offers prayers of praise, thanksgiving and intercession on behalf of the class, collectively and individually. The Prayer Leader leads the class in personal prayer by encouraging members to have daily prayer time. The Prayer Leader encourages members to maintain prayer journals where they record their prayer requests, as well as God's answers so they can know the power of prayer. This record keeping system helps us to remember how powerless we are and how powerful God is. "I can do all things through Christ which strengtheneth me." (Phil. 4:13)

The Prayer Leader's Duties

The Prayer Leader performs the following duties:

- Leads the class in praying daily for the specific needs of class members, prospects and the church.
- Requests praise reports, testimonies and prayer requests at each class gathering.
- Models how to conduct devotions in class fellowships and the home.
- Leads the class in participating in church wide prayer activities.
- Participates in the Fulfillment Hour Weekly Workers' Meetings.

The Prayer Leader's Gifts

The Prayer Leader employs these gifts:

- Intercession (Rom. 8:26-27, John 17:9-26, 1 Tim. 2:1-2, Col. 1:9-12, 4:12-13)
- Faith (1 Cor. 12:9, 13:2, Heb. 11:1, Rom. 4:18-21)
- Encouragement (Rom. 12:8, Acts 11:22-24, Acts 15:30-32)

Fulfillment Hour fulfills the purposes of God by using praise and prayer to prepare peoples' hearts for worship.

THE POWER OF ENROLLMENT
NUMBERS AT WORK

"Then they that gladly received his word were baptized: and the same day there were added unto them about three thousand souls."—Acts 2:41

Fulfillment Hour is a powerful tool that can be used to grow any church in any denomination. ***There is a direct relationship between the growth of Fulfillment Hour and the growth of your church.***

God works through people. Every Fulfillment Hour enrollment number represents a person in whose life God is working. As you watch your enrollment numbers grow, you are also watching your whole church grow.

The following Growth Pattern Chart shows that when emphasis is on Fulfillment Hour enrollment, the total church program grows. Fulfillment Hour undergirds worship and all other ministries by helping people find their places in the body of Christ, teaching them the importance of edifying the body and encouraging them to serve God with their gifts.

FULFILLMENT HOUR GROWTH PATTERN CHART

**When emphasis is on Fullfillment Hour enrollment,
the entire church grows.**

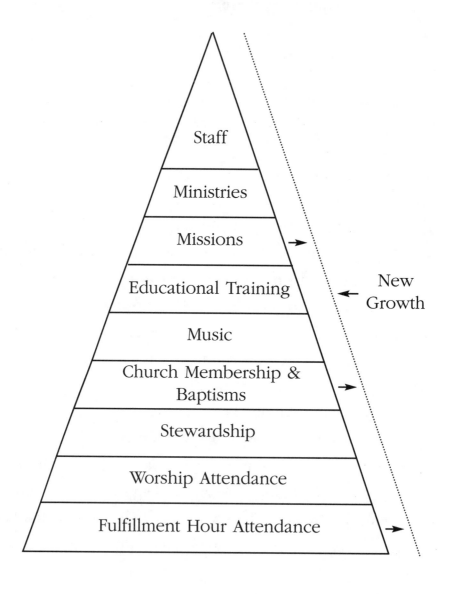

The Fulfillment Hour class grows through enrollment. Increased enrollment increases:

(1) Fulfillment Hour Attendance: The attendance increases as your enrollment increases. The more people you have enrolled, the more people will attend Fulfillment Hour.

(2) Baptisms: Increased enrollment adds new opportunities for evangelism and increases the number of converts.

(3) Offerings: Surveys reveal that those attending Sunday School contribute the majority of the offerings.

Open Enrollment

Open enrollment must be practiced at all times. Open enrollment is the process of enrolling anyone, any place, anytime as members of Fulfillment Hour, as long as he/she agrees. *The person has to agree to be enrolled in a Fulfillment Hour class.* To enroll a preschooler, child or youth, we must first get the parent's or guardian's permission.

> Open enrollment is the process of enrolling anyone, any place, anytime as members of Fulfillment Hour, as long as he/she agrees.

An enrollment is not an enrollment unless we have the individual's name, address and phone number. If the enrollee is a child, we must also have the parent's or guardian's name and the child's birthdate. Without all this necessary information, we have a "prospect"—not an enrollment.

Set Enrollment Goals

If you want to grow, you must make a conscious effort to do so. Until you set the vehicle in motion with clear goals, dreams will remain wishes. In Habakkuk 2:2, God tells us to "write the vision and make it plain." Set an enrollment goal based on real numbers. Get input from each class, department and division. Then, make sure everyone knows the goal you are working toward. *An untold goal is a defeatist attitude.*

Things happen when you have a goal. Goals keep everyone on track and they reinforce everyone's determination to succeed. Everyone who is involved experiences a sense of satisfaction and accomplishment. Everyone grows in faith and grace. Most importantly, the

> *The key is to set numerical goals, then have specific things to do to help you accomplish these goals.*

vision of what God wants to be done is achieved and expanded. The key is to set numerical goals, then have specific things to do to help you accomplish these goals. (See Appendix 16 for sample Fulfillment Hour goals.)

Some Ways to Increase the Enrollment

Enrollment grows when the Shepherd and the class members start to visit, make contacts, pray for, witness to and disciple new members. Let's explore some ways to increase your enrollment.

- Make enrollment a priority.
- Adopt an open enrollment approach.
- Create a prospect file and set a goal for the number you desire on file.
- Enroll guests the first time they attend or contact and visit them later.
- Enroll new members when they join the church.
- Organize a Pastor's class for new members only, and then convert each group of new members into a separate new class. *(Note: This is how you assimilate new members who join the church through the worship experience instead of through Fulfillment Hour.)*
- Use the enrollment list from Vacation Bible School to identify and invite prospects.
- Celebrate achievements. Enthusiasm is contagious. When people see the success and excitement surrounding Fulfillment Hour, they will want to become a part of it too.

- Conduct a "Soul-Winning Workshop" two times each month.
- Enroll everywhere you go.
- Work with overflowing enthusiasm!

Enrollment Strategies

Guest Cards

Gather the guest cards from Sunday's worship service. Everyone who completed a guest card should receive a call from Fulfillment Hour. The caller states: "Hello, I am Mary Doe from (name) Church, and I am calling on behalf of the Pastor and the entire church family. We thank God for your presence on yesterday." (Pause and listen) Then explain that one does not have to be a member of the church to enroll in Fulfillment Hour. Ask, "May we enroll you and your family in our Fulfillment Hour?" If the answer is yes, then complete an enrollment card for each family member. Be sure to complete all information on the enrollment card. If the answer is no, thank the person for visiting and invite them to worship and Fulfillment Hour.

Worship Service and Special Sundays

During Sunday worship service, when your church typically has a large number of people, ask the Pastor to explain to the congregation how the Fulfillment Hour is the infrastructure and delivery system of the church. He should then ask for a show of hands of those who are not enrolled and would like to be enrolled. Have enrollment cards ready for the ushers to hand out. (Use cardstock in a distinctive color. This will make them easy to identify and file.) Expect to receive a high number of enrollment cards.

Literature

Using the Fulfillment Hour literature is a good way to add numbers. Deliver a learner's guide to prospects from the Sunday morning guest cards, marking the page for the following Sunday's lesson. While there, invite them to a Fulfillment Hour class. Promise the person that he/she will not be asked to read or pray when he/she comes to Fulfillment Hour.

Twinning

After you implement the strategies described above, expect growth. In fact, you can expect the kind of growth that will result in your classes growing into "twins." Each adult Fulfillment Hour class is expected to reproduce itself in what we call a *twinning* process. The challenge of twinning is it requires us to abandon our comfort zones by leaving our current Fulfillment Hour classes and start-

> *Each adult Fulfillment Hour class is expected to reproduce itself in what we call a twinning process.*

ing new ones. However, the temporary discomfort is worth the reward. Twinning is how we empower new leaders and start new classes.

The twinning process is as follows:

Step 1. Enlist an Apprentice in each adult Fulfillment Hour class. The Apprentice is enlisted in accordance to the same procedure as enlisting Shepherds. (See "Enlisting Shepherds" in Chapter 14.)

Step 2. Enroll the Apprentices in the next Potential Workers' Training. (See Chapter 13.) Create an accelerated class, if necessary.

Step 3. On the "birthday" of the new class, the Apprentice (who has completed training) takes 6–12 class missionaries (including someone to serve as Secretary, Care Group Leader, Prayer Leader and Outreach Leader) to start the new class.

Step 4. The Apprentice becomes the Shepherd of the newly created class.

Step 5. The missionaries remain with the new class for approximately three months or until the class becomes established with new individuals to fulfill these class positions. The missionaries can then go back to their original class or may choose to remain with the new class.

In conclusion, enrollment numbers are important and can work for you when you follow the leadership actions of Jesus. Jesus knew His mission and developed a plan. He formed a team to carry out the plan. He trained the team and kept the goal/mission before the team. He prayed and spent time with them. He forgave them when they made mistakes. He allowed them to be leaders and kept them informed. He loved them until the end.

TRAINING IS THE KEY

*"Study to show thyself approved unto God, a workman that needeth
not to be ashamed, rightly dividing the word of truth."*
—2 Timothy 2:15

Trained workers are essential to having an effective Fulfillment Hour. Actually, *there are no trained workers, only workers in training.* Initial and ongoing training must be provided to all Fulfillment Hour workers. The following table lists the recommended training curriculum. A description of the courses follows.

Position	Courses	Frequency Offered
All Positions	Potential Workers' Training	Semi-annually
	Positional Training	Monthly
Shepherd	Workers' Meeting	Weekly
Evangelism/ Outreach Leader	Soul-Winning Workshop	Semi-monthly
Discipleship Leader	Discipleship Train-the-Trainer	Monthly

Potential Workers' Training

This course is required for all workers. It is typically an eight-week class in which a separate topic is taught each week. (See Appendix 17 for a sample course outline.) The topics include:

(1) Growth-Oriented Sunday School (GOSS)

(2) Modeling the Process of Teaching

(3) Fulfilling the Purposes of the Church Through a Growth-Oriented Sunday School

(4) How to Reach and Teach (age level training for adult, preschool, children and youth)

(5) Evangelism Training (Soul-Winning Workshop and Evangelism Blitz)

(6) Discipleship Training

(7) Secretary's Training

(8) Traits of Effective Teaching

Positional Training

Once a month, positional breakout sessions are conducted in the Weekly Workers' Meeting for the Outreach/Evangelism Leaders, Discipleship Leaders, Fellowship Leaders, Ministry Project Leaders, Missions Leaders, Prayer Leaders, Care Group Leaders and Secretaries. The training is specialized for each position. A church ministry leader in each of the areas conducts the sessions. The facililator uses the position descriptions to train the positional leaders. Members also share experiences at this time and they learn from each other. For example, Prayer Leaders from the Adult Division come together to learn how to be effective and share prayer concerns.

Weekly Workers' Meeting

These weekly leadership meetings are designed to help all Fulfillment Hour leaders be more effective in all aspects of the *church-at-work*. A regular meeting time allows Fulfillment Hour leaders to focus on the mission of the church and on relationships with each other. The meetings cover

> These weekly leadership meetings are designed to help all Fulfillment Hour leaders be more effective in all aspects of the church-at-work.

administrative concerns and include a review of the upcoming Sunday's lesson by a Master Shepherd.

The Weekly Workers' Meetings are used for leadership development and should be given priority. We recommend that no other meeting is scheduled during this time. The Workers' Meetings provide an opportunity to model the principles you want the workers to carry into their classes. The Prayer Leaders should lead the devotion. A "community time" activity should be planned to help leaders get to know each other. Recognition should be given to celebrate individual contributions as well as those things that are being done well. After addressing matters that concern everyone, the divisions may have separate breakouts to review and prepare for the upcoming Sunday's lesson. At least monthly, the breakout sessions should include positional training.

A suggested agenda follows. Our Fulfillment Hour Workers' Meetings at Greenforest are described in an article that appeared in the January 2002 issue of *Sunday School Leadership Magazine* (Appendix 18).

Fulfillment Hour Sample Workers' Meeting Agenda

Date
Time

DEVOTION   Prayer Leaders

WELCOME   Superintendent

COMMUNITY TIME   Superintendent

SECRETARY'S REPORT   FH Secretary
Enrollment: Attendance: Contacts:
Shared Christ: Received Christ:
New Enrollees: Drops:

ANNOUNCEMENTS:
- List dates & times for upcoming events over the next month.
- List major events that may be several months out, but require planning now.
- Include important reminders and/or exceptions to the normal calendar of activities.

TIP OF THE WEEK (Words of Inspiration)

"God loves you and longs for you to come into His presence so He can fill you with peace and strength."

Fulfillment Hour Sample Workers' Meeting Agenda
(cont'd)

FH BUSINESS   Minister of Christian
(Includes recognition)   Education

DIVISIONAL/POSITIONAL BREAKOUT

LESSON REVIEW   Adult Master
                                                      Shepherd

CLOSING PRAYER   Prayer Leader

Soul-Winning Workshop

The Soul-Winning Workshop teaches every Fulfillment Hour worker how to witness to others. The objective of the workshop is for leaders to understand and accept our Christian responsibility to evangelize. The workshop provides them an opportunity to practice sharing their personal testimonies and discuss their fears and apprehension in a safe, supportive environment. We recommend combining the Soul-Winning Workshop with a witnessing project, e.g., an Evangelism Blitz so they can immediately apply what they learned.

Discipleship Train-the-Trainer

The purpose of the Discipleship Train-the-Trainer is to prepare the Discipleship Leaders to teach the small study groups. ***This training is only necessary if all of the study groups will be studying the same topic and you wish to maintain consistency of message.*** The training may be conducted by anyone who is qualified to train others on the subject, e.g., the Pastor, the Minister of Discipleship or an experienced Discipleship Leader.

Training Resources

Listed below are additional training resources that you may find helpful:

Books

Stir Up the Gifts by Dr. George o. McCalep, Sr.

Seven Laws of the Learner by Bruce Wilkinson

Growing Up to the Head by Dr. George O. McCalep, Jr.

The Joshua Ministry: God's Witnessing Army by Rev. David
   Hopewell, Sr.

Sin in the House by Dr. George O. McCalep, Jr.

Workshops and Conferences

Check with your Ministers of Discipleship and Christian Education to identify workshops and conferences that are available through your local church and your denomination's headquarters. These may include regional and national conventions.

We invite you to join us at Greenforest's **Ministry Fest** conference. It is hosted at our church in Decatur, Georgia, during the second week of July. It is a wonderful opportunity for ministers and lay people to receive practical instruction on how to *do church God's way*. Visit our web site at www.greenforest.org to learn more about Ministry Fest.

Also, the authors as well as our pastor, Dr. George O. McCalep, Jr. are available to conduct workshops and seminars at your local church. Call 404-486-6740 for scheduling information.

Challenges

Some of the challenges facing Fulfillment Hours workers include:

- Low morale
- Shortened terms of service
- High absenteeism
- Limited opportunities for beginning new classes and departments
- Poor attendance at Weekly Workers' Meetings
- Inaccurate and incomplete records, etc.

How do you overcome these challenges? Proper enlistment followed by effective training and assimilation is the key. (See Chapter 14 and the Enlistment Skit in Appendix 8 for the dos and don'ts of enlistment.). Here are some enlistment tips:

(1) Ask each worker (including Shepherds) to complete a profile that lists his/her spiritual gifts. (See Appendix 5 for a sample Worker Profile.) *That means they have to know what their spiritual gifts are.* If they do not know what their gifts are, recommend they attend spiritual gifts training.

(2) Encourage teamwork between the Coordinator/ Directors, Department Directors and workers in each division.

(3) Make sure new Shepherds know how to use the curriculum materials and other resources effectively.

(4) Assign experienced workers to mentor new workers.

(5) Ask each leader to sign a commitment form each year committing to serve for a minimum of one year. *This should not be difficult because Christians are committed people.*

Assessing Training Needs

Ongoing training is essential for your Fulfillment Hour workers to grow professionally and maintain enthusiasm for their work. You can ensure that your ongoing training is effective by periodically assessing their training needs. Here's how:

(1) Evaluate training that is already in place. (See "Evaluating Training" below.)

(2) Observe all classes/units.

(3) Distribute a training needs survey.

(4) Summarize and prioritize the training needs.

(5) Implement a strategy to meet the training needs.

Evaluating Training

An observation is an opportunity to catch people doing something right. It is a tool to help the Shepherd and the Fulfillment Hour Director maximize resources and share effective teaching techniques. Here are some guidelines to follow when conducting observations:

(1) The *observer* should have some official status, e.g., Department Director, Director of Teaching Improvement and Training Coordinator/Director, Superintendent, etc.

(2) The Shepherd and the observer should agree on an observation date in advance. They should also talk about the things to which the Shepherd would like the observer to pay particular attention.

(3) On the day of the observation, the observer should arrive early and not draw attention to himself.

(4) The observer should make mental notes while the class is in progress, then write down what he/she observed as soon as the session is over. If there is a fear of forgetting something, then discreetly jot it down during the class. (See Sample Class Observation Form in Appendix 19.)

(5) At a mutually agreeable time, the Shepherd and observer should have a follow-up conference to discuss the observer's feedback.

When observing and evaluating classes/units, notice the following:

(1) Is the Shepherd modeling the process of teaching?

(2) Is the department staffed properly?

(3) Is the Bible being used?

(4) Are the curriculum materials being used correctly?

(5) Who is present and who is absent?

(6) How much teaching is taking place?

(7) Are members involved in the teaching?

(8) What is the general attitude of the workers on Sunday morning?

(9) What needs to be improved?

(10) What about space? Does the class need a smaller or larger room?

Training is the "key to spiritual growth." Proper enlistment and effective training are the keys to having servants versus volunteers. A volunteer looks upon teaching as another commitment he/she is obligated to fulfill. However, Isaiah 6:8 states, "Also I heard the voice of the Lord saying, whom shall I send, and who will go for us? Then said I, Here

Training is the "key to spiritual growth."

am I; send me." These are the words of a servant. When your Fulfillment Hour workers are properly matched to the place in the body of Christ where their passion lies, using the spiritual gifts that God has given them and performing the tasks that God has called them to, you will have people who have a servant's mentality. What's the difference in servants and volunteers? Bugbee, Cousins, and Hybels explain it this way in their book, *Network*:

Perspectives	Volunteers...	Servants...
Serve out of:	Obligation	Obedience
Are motivated to serve by a concern for:	What others see	What God sees
Serve with the attitude of:	"It's not my job."	"Whatever it takes."
Have a ministry mindset that says:	"Me first."	"Father first."
Serves with a Spirit of:	Pride	Humility
Results are:	Self-seeking	God-glorifying

What Can a Training Program Do for a Growing Fulfillment Hour?

(1) Build confidence.

(2) Provide inspiration.

(3) Give direction.

(4) Equip people to assume leadership roles.

(5) Teach people the Bible skillfully and properly.

(6) Build teams and increase teamwork.

(7) Help the worker understand the job he/she is asked to perform.

(8) Help the Shepherd understand the learners he/she teaches.

(9) Benefit both the church and Fulfillment Hour.

THE EMPLOYMENT AGENCY OF THE CHURCH

CHAPTER 14

"For we are his workmanship, created in Christ Jesus unto good works, which God hath before ordained that we should walk in them."—Eph. 2:10

As the employment agency of the church, our goal must continue to be obedience to the Great Commission (Matt. 28:19-20). Jesus challenges His followers in the Great Commission to emphasize three actions:

(1) Going

(2) Evangelizing

(3) Discipling

Where can these three actions be fulfilled? ***Fulfillment Hour is the place and its participants and leaders are the people to carry out the Great Commission.*** Fulfillment Hour enables the church to live up to its purpose by being the church's employment agency. Fulfillment Hour should have one of the largest number of participants, leaders and workers of any ministry of the church.

How Does it Work?

As an employment agency, the Fulfillment Hour matches positions and responsibilities with workers and leaders. The Fulfillment Hour employs people to work on church-wide evangelism, discipleship, fellowship, ministry and mission projects, and in the Fulfillment Hour ministry.

> *As an employment agency, the Fulfillment Hour matches positions and responsibilities with workers and leaders.*

In Chapters 7–11, we discussed how Fulfillment Hour fulfills the purposes of God through evangelism, discipleship, fellowship, ministry/missions and worship. We will not reiterate all that. Instead, we will use the following table to briefly summarize how Fulfillment Hour employs people in these functions of the church.

Church Function	Fulfillment Hour...
Evangelism	• Provides people to go witnessing.
Discipleship	• Encourages people to attend Bible Study and participate in all discipleship training.
Fellowship	• Builds loving relationships and assimilates new members.
Ministry	• Identifies needs among church members and prospects. • Provides workers to support ministry projects targeted at members of the church.

Church Function	Fulfillment Hour...
Missions	• Provides support for local, national and international missions to serve people who are outside of the local church. • Identifies needs of prospects who are not members of the church.
Worship	• Prepares the hearts of the people for worship through praise and prayer.

Enlisting Shepherds

We know that to whom much is given, much is required (Luke 12:48). In today's world, we must be in a posture of prevention when enlisting people to work with children. We have developed the following process for enlisting Shepherds and any persons who may encounter preschoolers, children or youth:

Step 1. The prospective Shepherd (worker) expresses a desire to work in Fulfillment Hour to the Fulfillment Hour Administration or is recommended by the Pastor, Shepherd or another worker.

Step 2. The prospective Shepherd (worker) personally schedules an interview with the Pastor or his designee. The interviewer has the opportunity to discover if the individual's beliefs are theologically sound. During the interview, the Pastor or his designee discusses and completes the following forms with the prospective Shepherd (worker). (See Appendices 4, 5 and 6 for samples of the forms.)

Adult Workers	Preschool, Children's and Youth Workers
• Leadership Requirements Checklist • Worker Profile	• Leadership Requirements Checklist • Worker Profile • Servant Leader Form

Step 3. A criminal background check is conducted through local, state and federal law enforcement agencies for people desiring to work with preschoolers, children and/or youth.

Step 4. The prospective worker completes the Potential Workers' Training.

Step 5. The prospective worker is officially awarded the title *Shepherd* when he/she meets all of the requirements.

Step 6. The Shepherd signs the "Commitment Covenant" (Appendix 7) agreeing to serve for a minimum of one year.

Enlisting Positional Leaders

Follow these steps when enlisting positional leaders other than Shepherds:

Step 1. Pray. Seek the Lord's leadership and claim the promise of Matthew 9:38.

Step 2. Ask these questions:

(a) Will the church accept this person as a Fulfillment Hour worker?

(b) Can this person serve, if willing? This question has to be answered by the individual being enlisted.

Step 3. Make an appointment with the person you want to enlist. Tell the person why you want to talk to him/her. It is best to talk with them face-to-face.

Step 4. Explain the responsibilities of the job. Give the person a written job description and other material that is pertinent to the job for which he/she is being enlisted.

Step 5. Discuss the expectations related to attending the Weekly Workers' Meetings, setting goals and signing the workers' Commitment Covenant (Appendix 7).

Step 6. Provide resources, e.g., Fulfillment Hour literature, supplies, upcoming training opportunities and prayer support.

Step 7. Answer the enlistee's questions.

Step 8. Ask the enlistee to pray to determine where the Lord would have him or her serve.

For a demonstration of the proper and improper ways of enlisting workers, see the skit, "Enlistment in Action" in Appendix 8.

Other Fulfillment Hour Workers

Workers are needed to assist the Fulfillment Hour Administration with other responsibilities that go beyond the regular positions in each Fulfillment Hour class. These responsibilities may be combined with or filled by current positions. Additional workers are needed to:

- Study and update space needs for the classes.
- Study divisional furnishings and equipment needs and make recommendations to the Fulfillment Hour Administration.
- Monitor the Fulfillment Hour budget and verify that there are adequate funds for literature, supplies and other needed items. (See the sample budget in Appendix 9.)
- Personally enlist workers.
- Coordinate Potential Workers' Training.
- Advertise Fulfillment Hour training sessions and meetings.
- Coordinate the annual appreciation banquet. (See "Annual Appreciation Banquet" in Chapter 16.)

- Help collect and summarize the weekly Attendance Records from each class/unit/department on Sunday mornings. (We call these workers "Office Assistants.")

Handling Ineffective Workers

There are numerous reasons why workers are ineffective. Several common reasons are:

(1) Spiritual immaturity (Sometimes this is discovered in the interview process with the Pastor.)

(2) Shortsightedness or lack of vision

(3) Poor enlistment (Expectations and responsibilities were inadequately explained.)

(4) No or poor training

(5) Not placed to serve within their spiritual gift(s)

(6) Lack of motivation (This can be the result of any of the other reasons.)

(7) Health challenges

(8) Personal problems

The best way to minister to ineffective workers is to take the following steps to *prevent them from becoming one*:

(1) Clarify expectations and responsibilities up front and throughout the training process.

(2) Train effectively. Be thorough and clear regarding all responsibilities.

(3) Encourage faithfully. Help them believe in themselves until they feel confident and competent.

(4) Exhort excellence.

(5) Hold everyone accountable for his/her actions.

When it is necessary to counsel people who are ineffective in their positions, follow these guidelines:

(1) Seek to understand the cause of their problems.

(2) Pray for discernment and wisdom.

(3) Pray for them to be receptive to your help.

(4) Fire them up before you fire them out.

(5) Consider the spiritual well-being of the entire group/class/unit.

(6) Pray that God will change their hearts and give them a desire to serve.

(7) When all else fails and the workers feel no need for improvement and are unwilling to change, relieve them of their responsibilities.

MOTIVATIONAL IDEAS FOR LEADERS

"I can do all things through Christ which strengtheneth me."
—Phil. 4:13

Obedience to the Great Commission should be the reason behind motivating church leaders. Fulfillment Hour serves as one of the strongest ministries for carrying out the Great Commission. The purpose of this chapter is to give motivational ideas to church leaders and congregations in all areas of church life. The only thing we ask is an open mind. Motivation can be extrinsic as well as intrinsic. However, when a climate of motivation is created, Fulfillment Hour workers are inspired to do their best. There are several ways this can be facilitated.

Motivation From the Administration

First, *workers feel good and work better when they have sufficient space to do their job.* The Administration should be committed to providing proper space and equipment. According to author Neil Jackson, it takes 12-square feet of floor space for each youth and adult in attendance. It takes 25–30 square feet of floor space for preschoolers and children. If the classroom is too small, learning is compromised because everyone is uncomfortable.

Secondly, the Administration should listen to and support departmental projects by providing funds and attending their respective functions, e.g., the Preschool Division's "Doughnuts for Dads" function on Father's Day.

Thirdly, encourage and publicly recognize workers when they complete a project. An example is if the Children's Division workers were traveling to a church that had experienced a major disaster, the Administration should see the group off as they depart and take pictures to later display and discuss in the Weekly Workers' Meeting. Upon their return the workers should be praised for the specific work they did, e.g., providing clothes and toys for the children or assisting the church in other areas of need.

> *The Administration should listen to and support departmental projects by providing funds and attending their respective functions.*

Finally, ***recognition should be a standard agenda item for all gatherings, especially at the Weekly Workers' Meeting.*** An annual appreciation banquet should be held to recognize workers at the unit/class, departmental and divisional levels. (See "Annual Appreciation Banquet" in Chapter 16.)

Motivation From the Pulpit

The most powerful place to promote from is the pulpit. The most powerful person to do promotion is the Pastor. The Pastor's voice from the pulpit has the greatest influence on the greatest number of people. When workers hear the Pastor talking about, and see him actively involved in Fulfillment Hour, they feel that they are a part of something that is important to the church and its ministry.

> *The most powerful place to promote from is the pulpit. The most powerful person to do promotion is the Pastor. The Pastor's voice from the pulpit has the greatest influence on the greatest number of people.*

Recognition Motivates!

Recognize people for what you want them to do. If we want people to visit and make contacts, we must give recognition when it is done. To be effective, recognition must be immediate, i.e., it should occur as close to the accomplishment as possible. For example, when giving recognition for the number of new members enrolled, do not wait until the end of the month. Report it at the next Weekly Workers' Meeting. Do not say, "We had six new members." Instead, call the person who did the enrolling by name. Say, "The class of 'John the Baptist,' shepherded by Brother John Doe, had six new members. Let's give the Lord a hand!"

Motivating Yourself

While you are working hard to keep everyone else fired up, don't forget about yourself.

(1) Work on your attitude.

(2) Build faith in yourself. "If you have faith as a grain of mustard seed, you shall say unto this mountain, remove hence to yonder place; and it shall remove and nothing shall be impossible unto you." (Matt. 17:20)

> While you are working hard to keep everyone else fired up, don't forget about yourself.

(3) Stay positive. "Thou wilt keep him in perfect peace, whose mind is stayed on thee." (Isaiah 26:3)

(4) Keep a pen and notepad by your bedside. When you wake up at night with ideas, immediately write them down.

(5) Be a list maker. Lists give you directions for the day and establish priority levels and values about what you give your time to. You will have a great sense of accomplishment as you check things off your list.

(6) Set smart goals. "Where there is no vision, the people perish." (Prov. 29:18) If the leadership of a church does not know where it wants to go, how can a congregation? To have a healthy Fulfillment Hour and, thus a healthy church, set goals that

directly support your vision. Goals should be set in the areas of:

(a)   Enrollment

(b)   Attendance

(c)   Potential Workers' Training graduates

(d)   New units/classes

(e)   Weekly Workers' Meeting attendance

(f)   Baptisms

(g)   Leadership Development

(7)   Establish positive reading habits. Read material that will build your mindset and increase positive thinking.

(8)   Practice associating with positive, energetic, enthusiastic people.

(9)   Avoid negative thoughts, negative conversation and negative company.

(10) Write your vision and read it regularly. "Make it plain upon the tables, that he may run that readeth it." (Hab. 2:2)

Motivating Your Class

The Fulfillment Hour Shepherd has the responsibility of motivating her class. A learner feels good knowing that his Shepherd actually knows his name. While the Shepherd should know his learners' names, the Shepherd is expected to know and do much, much more. Learners get a sense of how much

> A learner feels good knowing that his Shepherd actually knows his name.

the Shepherd cares about them by their level of professionalism and commitment to the class. If you want to motivate your class, we recommend practicing the following behaviors:

- Know the characteristics of the class level you are teaching. This knowledge directs the way that the Shepherd communicates and motivates his class.
- Know personal information about the learners.
- Know the spiritual level of the learners.
- Contact the learners on a regular basis.
- Encourage each learner's growth.
- Make a point of coming to class on time.
- Come to class prepared.
- Involve the class in discussion. Do not lecture constantly.
- Do not cancel class when you cannot be there. Arrange for a substitute Shepherd.

As a result of all of the above, the class members should feel motivated to come to class, become active in the class and give God their very best service.

Motivational Ideas Used in Our Fulfillment Hour

We have had tremendous success employing various motivational strategies at Greenforest over the years. Here are a few ideas that have worked really well.

- Enlist a greeter in your class to make sure all guests and new members are welcomed.
- Have community time in each class in order to make lasting friendships. (See Chapter 9.)
- Twin (reproduce) your adult class when it reaches an enrollment of 25 or more. This will keep the size of your class small so that new members will be wanted and involved. (The twinning process is described in Chapter 12 under "Twinning.")
- Assign every member to a Care Group Leader.
- Make sure the Fellowship Leader understands the importance of her role in assimilating new members.
- Follow up and through with prospects and new members.
- Celebrate special occasions, e.g., birthdays, weddings, births, graduations, job promotions, etc.
- Immediately enroll prospects and new members in a Fulfillment Hour class or department.

- Disciple class members by forming small study groups (as small as two members) using the book *Growing Up to the Head* by Dr. George McCalep, Jr.

- Minister to and involve the entire family in all fellowship activities.

- Help members discover their spiritual gifts.

- Monitor your class records closely. This allows you to keep up with members of your class/department and assures that no one is "lost through the cracks."

- Enlist members to drive new members or guests to social activities or other church events.

- Use large print nametags.

- Form prayer partners in your class.

- Include motivational activities in all of your fellowship gatherings.

Jesus is the Fulfillment Hour model. He was the master motivator. Jesus went where the people were. He was concerned about people and He educated them. Jesus loved all the people. He knew the power of words and the power of silence. He shared His knowledge with the people and remained positive despite the circumstances. The goal of Fulfillment Hour is to motivate just as Jesus motivated others.

> *The goal of Fulfillment Hour is to motivate just as Jesus motivated others.*

CELEBRATE! CELEBRATE! CELEBRATE!

"Let every thing that hath breath praise the Lord. Praise ye the Lord."—Psalm 150:6

G iving recognition of service is a way to celebrate. We celebrate events, accomplishments and goal achievement. In this chapter, we will focus on five Fulfillment Hour events that we celebrate.

High Attendance Sunday

On a designated Sunday, all Fulfillment Hour classes/units make a point of inviting as many people as possible to attend Fulfillment Hour. This is referred to as *High Attendance Sunday*. High Attendance Sunday should be done quarterly to effectively increase attendance. High Attendance Sunday gives us an opportunity to mobilize all of our efforts to communicate pure concern for absentees, poor attendees, prospects and members.

High Attendance Sunday involves the entire Fulfillment Hour. Therefore, the entire Fulfillment Hour should be involved in planning for it. Every class becomes involved by setting two goals for High Attendance Sunday—contacts (number of invitations extended) and attendance. An announcement is given to each class to document their goals for High Attendance Sunday. See the following sample.

HIGH ATTENDANCE SUNDAY
SAMPLE ANNOUNCEMENT

March 10, XXXX is High Attendance Sunday. Our goal is to reach an attendance of _____ in Fulfillment Hour. Please share your plans with us to help reach this goal.

The _____ goal is to reach _____ in
        FH Class/Department   Number

attendance on March 10, XXXX. Our Contact Goal is _____.
                                                                              Number

Please return this form to the FH office TODAY.
(FEBRUARY 24, XXXX)

When High Attendance Sunday is over, we celebrate at the very next Weekly Workers' Meeting by giving recognition to all units and Shepherds who achieved their goals. Certificates are given to the class/unit and department that fulfilled both their attendance and contact goals. (See sample Goal-Reaching Certificate in Appendix 21.)

Starting two Sundays before the event, testimonies are given during worship service to promote High Attendance Sunday. A Fulfillment Hour member is asked to share his/her testimony as to how the Fulfillment Hour has helped him/her grow as a Christian. High Attendance Day is also promoted at the Weekly Workers' Meeting. (See special article about Leadership Meetings in the January 2002 issue of *Leadership Magazine* in Appendix 18.)

Below are some other strategies to use in promoting High Attendance Sunday:

(1) Have each class set realistic attendance goals. Goals should be simple and measurable, yet challenging and reasonable. The entire class (workers and students) should be involved in setting the goal.

(2) Encourage class members to take part in achieving the goal. The Great Commission was given to all believers. Therefore, we are all Care Group and Outreach Leaders.

(3) Ask the Pastor to announce High Attendance Sunday from the pulpit for at least two consecutive Sundays prior to the event.

(4) Use a variety of media or methods to promote High Attendance Sunday. Be creative! Some examples are:

(a) Distribute fliers. (See Appendix 20.)

(b) Write letters to prospects with details about what the class is studying.

(c) Swap prospect/member lists with another class.

(d) Contact parents who regularly send their children to Fulfillment Hour, but do not come themselves.

(e) Compile a list of unsaved and/or un-churched people from class members and send out invitations.

(f) Send postcards to new prospects who are not enrolled in Fulfillment Hour.

(g) Ask class members to invite friends, co-workers or family members who do not attend Fulfillment Hour on a regular basis.

(h) Look in the newspaper for weddings, newcomers to the neighborhood and job promotion announcements, and then send invitations to the people listed.

(5) Direct the campaign toward the audience you are trying to reach.

(6) Be enthusiastic in all undertakings.

(7) PRAY! PRAY! PRAY!

There are other strategies specifically for minors. The youth classes can send out postcards, conduct outreach blitzes, use entertainment or other group appeal functions. Children and preschool classes can "Bring-a-Friend" from school or their neighborhood, make handwritten postcard invitations or ask parents to help invite others. Parents can contact other parents and even arrange carpools.

Remember, the key to High Attendance Sunday is to **"GO F.I.S.H."**

F = Find (Search for people.)

I = Invite (Extend invitations via telephone calls or personal conversations.)

S = Share (Share Jesus with prospects and invite them to Fulfillment Hour.)

H = Harvest (Make all guests feel welcome. Make this an enjoyable time. Recognize their attendance. Invite them to other class fellowships.)

Annual Appreciation Banquet

Celebrate Fulfillment Hour with a banquet every year. Our banquet is on the first Saturday in November. When we started celebrating over 20 years ago, there were 12 people present. It has now grown to 350 in attendance. We are forever thankful to God.

Celebrate Fulfillment Hour with a banquet every year.

A Banquet Coordinator plans all of the banquet activities and keeps the Fulfillment Hour Administration informed. The banquet is a line item in the departmental budget. (See Appendix 9.)

A formal program is planned and awards are given. (See Appendix 22.) The Pastor presents the "Distinguished Awards" listed on the program. These Distinguished Awards include "Shepherd of the Year" for each division, the "Servantship Award" and the "Spirit Award." The Distinguished Award recipients receive plaques. However, many other certificates can be given to recognize every significant contribution that was made during the year. Some of our awards are:

- Evangelism Award
- Discipleship Leader Award
- Prayer Leader(s) Award
- Mission Project Award
- Ministry Project Award
- Workers' Meeting Attendance Award
- Contact Award
- Longevity Award
- "Quality Plus" Award
- "Extra Special" Award
- "Thanks for All You Do" Award
- "Lesson Sharing" Award
- "We Appreciate You" Award

Potential Workers' Training Celebration/Recognition

Potential Workers' Training is a requirement for anyone interested in becoming a Fulfillment Hour worker. The end of the course is celebrated with a fun-filled fellowship. The person designated as the Fellowship Leader for the Potential Workers' class distributes a list of food and other items to the class. Class members sign their names next to the item they plan to bring. (See the Sample Fellowship Sign-up Sheet in Appendix 14.)

The Potential Workers' graduation ceremony is actually held at the Fulfillment Hour Annual Appreciation Banquet. Each graduate receives a special certificate. This is a very special occasion for the graduates because it is when *potential workers* officially become *Shepherds*.

Twinning Results Celebration

Twinned classes are special reasons to celebrate. We like to schedule all twinned classes to begin on a "Twinning Day." ***Every class that successfully twins itself is recognized and celebrated.*** Like always, the victory is given to God.

Fulfillment Hour Night at Revival

Most churches sponsor at least one revival each year. This is a very special and busy time for Fulfillment Hour. The first Monday of our revival is always dedicated as "Fulfillment Hour Night." This is a time when Fulfillment Hour really shines. Each class/unit, department and division proudly displays its banner. The banners can be anything from a single sheet of paper with the class name scrolled in crayon to an elaborate, professionally created full-sized banner. Some classes even have their own T-shirts that they wear.

As part of the celebration, our Pastor calls out each Fulfillment Hour division—Preschool, Children's, Youth and Adults. As he calls the division's name, Shepherds, workers and learners in each respective division stand with their banners. The group parades around the sanctuary with pride as the Pastor leads us in singing "Give Me That Old Fulfillment Hour Spirit" (in the tune of "Give Me That Old Time Religion"). After all divisions have been called, everybody in the sanctuary is on their feet giving praise to God for Fulfillment Hour. What a wonderful time!

EPILOGUE

URGENCY OF IMPLEMENTATION

"Watch therefore, for ye know neither the day nor the hour wherein the Son of man cometh."—Matt. 25:13

It is not enough to know, you must act and be held accountable for your actions! As Fulfillment Hour leaders, you must act to fulfill the purposes of God.

This book was designed to share the Greenforest Fulfillment Hour Model. The model does not belong to us. It belongs to God. God is its author and finisher. He used Pastor George O. McCalep, Jr. to carry the news of our responsibility to fulfill the purposes of God through Fulfillment Hour.

In the words of the Nike commercial, "Just do it!" The model has been developed. The organization has been structured. The position descriptions have been written. Fulfillment Hour has been tested and proven to work at Greenforest Community Baptist Church. It is currently being implemented in other churches across the country. As with other initiatives presented by God and implemented by man, there are those who may challenge its authenticity. There are those who feel, "We've always done it this way, so why do we need to change?" The answer again is, "This is not your granddaddy's Sunday School."

There is no time to wait. No man knows the day or the hour that the Lord will reappear (Matt. 24:36). Our marching orders are to get busy. There is a price for procrastination. In Haggai 1:5-6, 9-11, we are reminded that there is a price for putting off God's work. Failure to prioritize the work of the Kingdom results in frustration and disappointment. Faith and obedience is spiritual nourishment for believers. When we don't obey or live by faith, we end up undernourished. God is calling us today to be obedient to his Word.

It does not matter if your church is large or small, Black or White, rich or poor. It does not matter about your church's denomination or association. Fulfillment Hour is a model for Sunday Schools in any church. It is anticipated, and has been prophesied, that this model will revolutionize Sunday Schools' across this nation, and that an unparalleled Sunday School movement (revival) will break out.

Our only remaining suggestion is that before implementing any portion of this Fulfillment Hour model, pray, pray and pray some more. Then, remember to put God first and He will bless your good works through Jesus Christ.

BIBLIOGRAPHY

Anderson, Andy. *The Growth Spiral*. Broadman & Holman
    Publishers, Nashville, 1993.

Briscoe, Pete. *Christianity—A Follower's Guide*. Broadman &
    Holman Publishers, Nashville, 2001.

Bugbee, Bruce, Don Cousins and Bill Hybels. *Network: Participant's
    Guide*. Zondervan Publishing House, Grand Rapids, 1994.

Dean, Kenneth M. *Sunday School Handbook: Help for the Sunday
    School Director*. Convention Press, Nashville, 1992

Halley, H. H. *Halley's Bible Handbook*. Regency Reference Library,
    Michigan, 1965.

Hemphill, Ken. *Revitalizing the Sunday Morning Dinosaur*.
    Broadman & Holman Publishers, Nashville, 1996.

------ and Bill Taylor. *Ten Best Practices to Make Your Sunday School
    Work*. Lifeway Church Resources, Nashville, 2001.

Holy Bible. King James Version and New International Version.

Hopewell Sr., David. *The Joshua Ministry: God's Witnessing Army*.
    Orman Press, Lithonia, 2001.

Hunt, Josh. *You Can Double Your Class in Two Years or Less*. Group
    Publishing, Colorado, 1997.

Interviews with Joel Harrison. Lead association Missionary, Metro
    Atlanta Baptist Association.

Jackson, Neil E. Jr. *Doing the Impossible*. Broadman Press, 1985.

--------, *Motivational Ideas for Changing Lives*. Broadman Press, 1982.

Key Strategies for a Healthy Sunday School. Compiled and edited by Steve Parry, Bible Study Ministries, 2002.

McCalep Jr., George O. *Faithful Over a Few Things: Seven Critical Church Growth Principles*. Orman Press, Lithonia, 1996.

--------. *Growing Up to the Head: Ten Growth Essentials to Becoming a Better Christian*. Orman Press, Lithonia, 1997.

--------. *Sin in the House: Ten Crucial Church Problems with Cleansing Solutions*. Orman Press, Lithonia, 1999.

Mims, Gene. *Kingdom Principles for Church Growth*. Convention Press, Nashville, 1994.

Piland, Harry M. *Basic Sunday School Work*. Convention Press, Nashville, 1980.

--------. *Growing and Winning Through the Sunday School*. Convention Press, Nashville, 1981.

Poling, Wayne A. *Sunday School Leader Training Handbook*, Convention Press, Nashville, 1991.

Robinson, Darrell W. *People Sharing Jesus*. Thomas Nelson Publishers, Nashville, 1995.

Smith, Sid. *Ten Super Sunday Schools in the Black Community*. Broadman Press, Nashville, 1986.

Taylor, Bill L. *The Power to Change Lives: The Complete Guide for Building a Great Commission Sunday School.* Convention Press, Nashville, 1998.

------, and Louis B. Hanks. *Sunday School for a New Century.* Lifeway Press, Nashville, 1999.

Tiller, David and Larry Garner. *Teaching Like Jesus: Teaching that Really Changes Lives.* Members Resource. Sunday School Support Series, Volume 2.

INDEX OF APPENDICES

Permission is granted to reproduce any form appearing in this section.

APPENDIX 1

TEN WAYS TO HELP YOUR PASTOR
BECOME A FULFILLMENT HOUR PASTOR

1. Have a conference with your Pastor for prayer once a month. Thank God for him.

2. When appropriate, recognize your Pastor for becoming a "Fulfillment Hour Pastor." Give God the praise and thanks, but also give your Pastor credit.

3. Have your Pastor teach a class to all of the Fulfillment Hour workers, e.g., a book study.

4. Invite your Pastor and his wife for lunch or dinner in your home or take them out to dinner. Let your Pastor and First Lady know what a blessing it is to be under their leadership.

5. Never do anything that will embarrass your Pastor or the First Lady. Pray for your Pastor, his family and the church publicly as well as privately.

6. Ask your Pastor if he will help you start a Fulfillment Hour Weekly Workers' Meeting. If you already have one, invite your Pastor to attend.

7. Always give your Pastor concise information about the Fulfillment Hour, preferably one page at a time with one or two lines highlighted.

8. When meeting with your Pastor, have a short, written agenda. Never waste his time. The agenda should ask for his professional opinion, and not just tell him of your intentions.

9. Respect your Pastor's opinion. Remember that the Lord gives the vision to the Pastor.

10. Keep your Pastor informed. Ask him if he would announce from the pulpit something about the Fulfillment Hour every Sunday. Write the announcement out for him and always make it positive. Example: "We now have an enrollment of 100 members and 50 members were present in Fulfillment Hour this morning. Let's give the Lord a hand!"

APPENDIX 2

SAMPLE ADMINISTRATIVE ORGANIZATION
Adult Fulfillment Hour Division

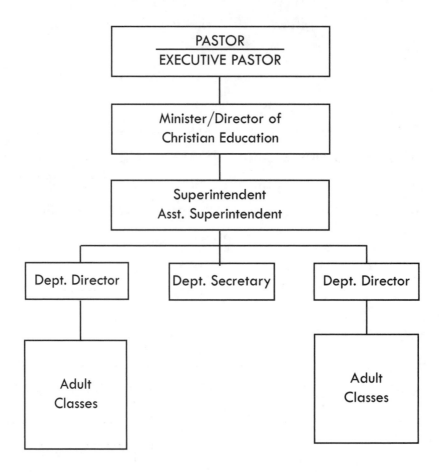

SAMPLE CLASS ORGANIZATIONAL CHART
Adult Fulfillment Hour Division

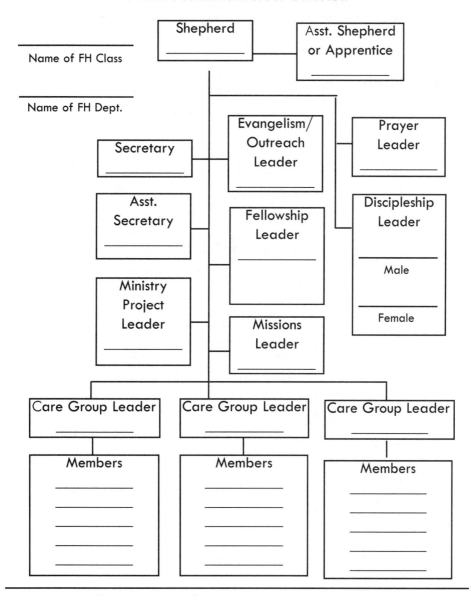

Name of FH Class

Name of FH Dept.

APPENDIX 2 (cont'd)

SAMPLE ORGANIZATIONAL CHART
Youth Fulfillment Hour Division

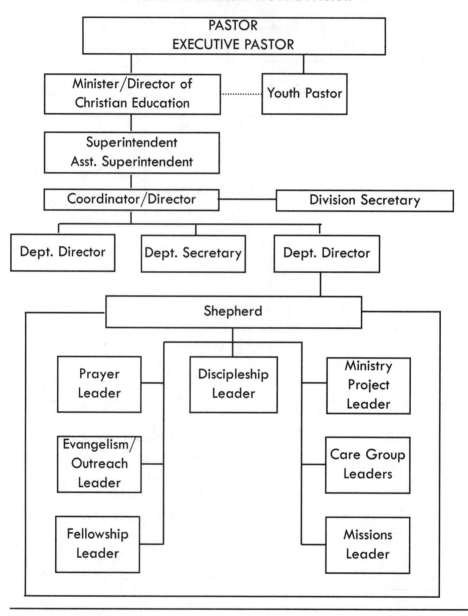

The class organization for the Youth Division is duplicated for each class within each department. The classes are structured to support a leader/learner attendance ratio of 1:12. The enrollment ratio may be 1:24 because attendance is usually 50% of enrollment.

Jr. High Department	**Sr. High Department**
7th Grade Girls	10th Grade
7th Grade Boys	11th Grade
8th Grade Girls	12th Grade
8th Grade Boys	
9th Grade Girls	
9th Grade Boys	

APPENDIX 2 (cont'd)

SAMPLE ORGANIZATIONAL CHART
Children's Fulfillment Hour Division

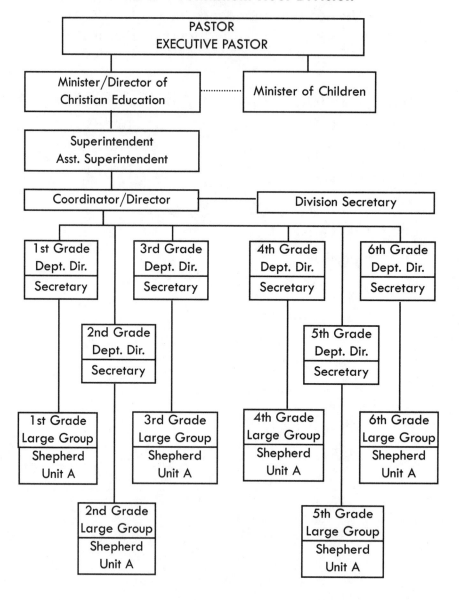

Each grade in the Children's Division has multiple units to support a leader/learner attendance ratio of 1:6. The enrollment ratio may be 1:12 because attendance is usually 50% of enrollment.

The Shepherd performs the function of Evangelism/Outreach, Discipleship, Fellowship, Prayer, Ministry/Missions and Care Group Leader unless these duties are assigned to other adult workers.

APPENDIX 2 (cont'd)

SAMPLE ORGANIZATIONAL CHART
Preschool Fulfillment Hour Division

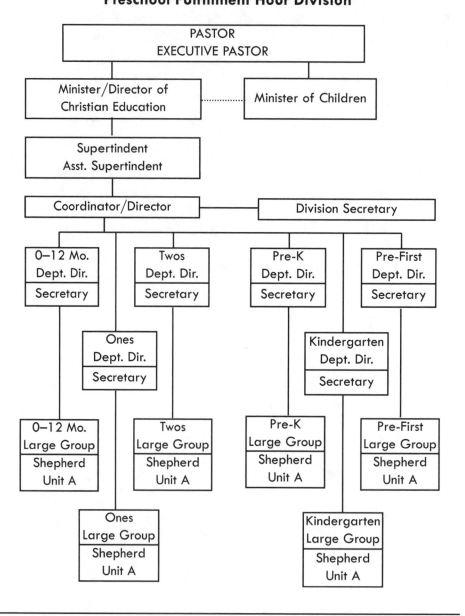

The Preschool Division has multiple units to support age appropriate leader/learner attendance ratios.

The Shepherd performs the function of Evangelism/Outreach, Discipleship, Fellowship, Prayer, Ministry/Missions and Care Group Leader unless these duties are assigned to other adult workers.

MINISTRY POSITION RESPONSIBILITIES

of the

FULFILLMENT HOUR MODEL

APPENDIX 3 (cont'd)

MINISTER/DIRECTOR of CHRISTIAN EDUCATION

The Minister/Director of Christian Education works with the Superintendent and Assistant Superintendent in planning, conducting and evaluating the work of Fulfillment Hour.

Duties

(1) Lead in determining the Fulfillment Hour organization needed to reach and teach effectively, including creating new classes/units as necessary.

(2) Oversee the enlistment of workers.

(3) Walk through the Fulfillment Hour campus with the Pastor monthly to ensure proper utilization of space and resources.

(4) Approve record changes/corrections before computer input.

(5) Inspect classes on Sunday mornings to ensure that all classes are properly in place and the Fulfillment Hour model is being followed.

(6) Implement and support the Fulfillment Hour model through evangelism, discipleship, fellowship, ministry and worship.

(7) Work with the Superintendent to compile a comprehensive annual budget.

(8) Work with the Superintendent to compile a comprehensive annual calendar.

(9) Give direction to the selection and proper use of all curriculum materials.

(10) Determine financial and physical resources needed for Fulfillment Hour and recommend the acquisition of those resources to the church.

(11) Analyze the Fulfillment Hour records to determine the proper course of action to develop growth.

(12) Lead in evaluating the work of Fulfillment Hour.

(13) Contact each Shepherd in Fulfillment Hour regularly to listen to concerns and solicit suggestions.

(14) Communicate with the Pastor, Coordinator/Directors, Minister of Youth and Children's Minister weekly to ensure quality.

APPENDIX 3 (cont'd)

SUPERINTENDENT

The Superintendent works with the Minister/Director of Christian Education and Assistant Superintendent in planning, conducting and evaluating the work of Fulfillment Hour.

<u>Duties</u>

(1) Lead in determining the Fulfillment Hour organization needed to reach and teach effectively.

(2) Give direction to the enlistment of workers for Fulfillment Hour.

(3) Give support and guidance to other Administration staff in accomplishing their work.

(4) Lead workers to become effective witnesses to unsaved persons.

(5) Implement and support the Fulfillment Hour model through evangelism, discipleship, fellowship, ministry and worship.

(6) Develop and maintain a Weekly Workers' Meeting.

(7) Work with the Minister/Director of Christian Education to compile a comprehensive annual budget.

(8) Work with the Minister/Director of Christian Education to compile a comprehensive annual calendar.

(9) Make sure that a Shepherd is in place in each class. When necessary, enlist substitute Shepherds or be prepared to fill-in.

(10) Coordinate the work of the Fulfillment Hour Secretary and Office Assistants.

(11) Analyze the Fulfillment Hour records for planning and improvement purposes.

(12) Lead in evaluating the work of Fulfillment Hour.

(13) Know the weekly Fulfillment Hour attendance and enrollment.

APPENDIX 3 (cont'd)

> ## ASSISTANT SUPERINTENDENT

The Assistant Superintendent works with the Minister/Director of Christian Education and Superintendent in planning, conducting and evaluating the work of Fulfillment Hour.

Duties

(1) Lead in evaluating the work of individual Fulfillment Hour classes.

(2) Fill-in as necessary in leading the Weekly Workers' Meeting.

(3) Assist in providing support and guidance to Fulfillment Hour workers in accomplishing their work.

(4) Assist the Fulfillment Hour Secretary and Office Assistants on Sunday mornings.

(5) Coordinate Fulfillment Hour tours guides for new members.

(6) Help implement and support the Fulfillment Hour model through evangelism, discipleship, fellowship, ministry and worship.

(7) Assist individuals who come to the Fulfillment Hour office looking for specific classes or individuals.

(8) Escort guests and/or new members to class locations.

(9) Assist in evaluating the work of Fulfillment Hour.

APPENDIX 3 (cont'd)

FULFILLMENT HOUR
SECRETARY

The Fulfillment Hour Secretary works with the Minister/Director of Christian Education, Superintendent and Assistant Superintendent in tracking all statistics that are relevant to Fulfillment Hour.

<u>Duties</u>

(1) Maintain the official composite enrollment of the entire Fulfillment Hour Ministry.

(2) Compile and maintain class records for all Fulfillment Hour classes, units, departments and divisions.

(3) Summarize the weekly Attendance Reports from each Fulfillment Hour class/unit.

(4) Compile all reports and statistics for Fulfillment Hour, including:
    a. Enrollment growth (year over year)
    b. Classes/units
    c. Attendance (weekly)
    d. Contacts (weekly)
    e. People with whom Christ was shared
    f. People accepting Christ
    g. Baptisms
    h. Guests

    i. Weekly Workers' Meeting Attendance
    j. Potential Workers' Training Graduates

(5) Maintain a list of workers in all positions.

(6) Maintain files of all forms that are completed and signed by all workers.

APPENDIX 3 (cont'd)

> # COORDINATOR/DIRECTOR
> ## Preschool Division

The Preschool Coordinator/Director works with the Fulfillment Hour Administration in planning, conducting and evaluating the work of the Preschool Division.

Duties

(1) Lead in determining the Fulfillment Hour organization needed for the Preschool Division to reach and teach effectively, including creating new units as necessary.

(2) Oversee the enlistment and training of workers for the Preschool Division.

(3) Walk through the Preschool Division campus monthly to give attention to Fulfillment Hour for motivational purposes.

(4) Approve all Preschool Division record changes/corrections.

(5) Inspect the Preschool departments on Sunday mornings to ensure that all classes are properly in place and the Fulfillment Hour model is being followed.

(6) Implement and support the Fulfillment Hour model in the Preschool Division through evangelism, discipleship, fellowship, ministry and worship.

(7) Compile and submit the annual budget for the Preschool Division to the Fulfillment Hour Administration.

(8) Compile and submit the annual calendar of activities for the Preschool Division to the Fulfillment Hour Administration.

(9) Give direction to the selection and proper use of all Preschool curriculum materials.

(10) Determine the financial and physical resources needed for the Preschool Division and make appropriate recommendations to the Fulfillment Hour Administration.

(11) Analyze the Preschool Division's records to determine the proper course of action to develop growth.

(12) Lead in evaluating the work of the Fulfillment Hour Preschool Division.

(13) Contact each Preschool Shepherd in Fulfillment Hour regularly to listen to concerns and solicit suggestions.

(14) Communicate with the Fulfillment Hour Administration on a weekly basis to ensure quality.

APPENDIX 3 (cont'd)

> # COORDINATOR/DIRECTOR
> ## Children's Division

The Children's Coordinator/Director works with the Fulfillment Administration in planning, conducting and evaluating the work of the Children's Division.

<u>Duties</u>

(1) Lead in determining the Fulfillment Hour organization needed for the Children's Division to reach and teach effectively, including creating new units as necessary.

(2) Oversee the enlistment and training of workers for the Children's Division.

(3) Walk through the Children's Division campus weekly to give attention to Fulfillment Hour for motivational purposes.

(4) Approve all Children's Division record changes/corrections.

(5) Inspect the Children's departments on Sunday mornings to ensure that all classes are properly in place and the Fulfillment Hour model is being followed.

(6) Implement and support the Fulfillment Hour model in the Children's Division through evangelism, discipleship, fellowship, ministry and worship.

(7) Compile and submit the annual budget for the Children's Division to the Fulfillment Hour Administration.

(8) Compile and submit the annual calendar of activities for the Children's Division to the Fulfillment Hour Administration.

(9) Give direction to the selection and proper use of all children's curriculum materials.

(10) Determine the financial and physical resources needed for the Children's Division and make appropriate recommendations to the Fulfillment Hour Administration.

(11) Analyze the records of the Children's Division to determine the proper course of action to develop growth.

(12) Lead in evaluating the work of the Fulfillment Hour Children's Division.

(13) Contact each Children's Division Shepherd in Fulfillment Hour regularly to listen to concerns and solicit suggestions.

(14) Communicate with the Fulfillment Hour Administration on a weekly basis to ensure quality.

APPENDIX 3 (cont'd)

COORDINATOR/DIRECTOR
Youth Division

The Youth Coordinator/Director works with the Fulfillment Hour Administration in planning, conducting and evaluating the work of the Youth Division.

<u>Duties</u>

(1) Lead in determining the Fulfillment Hour organization needed for the Youth Division to reach and teach effectively, including creating new classes as necessary.

(2) Oversee the enlistment and training of workers for the Youth Division.

(3) Walk through the Youth Division campus monthly to give attention to Fulfillment Hour for motivational purposes.

(4) Approve all Youth Division record changes/corrections.

(5) Inspect the Youth classes on Sunday mornings to ensure that all classes are properly in place and the Fulfillment Hour model is being followed.

(6) Implement and support the Fulfillment Hour model in the Youth Division through evangelism, discipleship, fellowship, ministry and worship.

(7) Compile and submit the annual budget for the Youth Division to the Fulfillment Hour Administration.

(8) Compile and submit the annual calendar of activities for the Youth Division to the Fulfillment Hour Administration.

(9) Give direction to the selection and proper use of all Youth curriculum materials.

(10) Determine the financial and physical resources needed for the Youth Division and make appropriate recommendations to the Fulfillment Hour Administration.

(11) Analyze the Youth Division's records to determine the proper course of action to develop growth.

(12) Lead in evaluating the work of the Fulfillment Hour Youth Division.

(13) Contact each Youth Shepherd in Fulfillment Hour regularly to listen to concerns and solicit suggestions.

(14) Communicate with the Fulfillment Hour Administration on a weekly basis to ensure quality.

APPENDIX 3 (cont'd)

DEPARTMENT DIRECTOR
Adult Division

The Department Director for the Adult Division works with the Fulfillment Hour Administration to disseminate and collect information. The Adult Department Director also helps to identify and address unexpected problems that may occur on Sunday mornings.

Duties

(1) Distribute the weekly class Attendance Records every Sunday morning to each class, pick them up at the end of the class period, summarize the attendance information and return the form to the Fulfillment Hour office.

(2) Maintain regular contact with the department's Shepherds.

(3) Disseminate information to the Shepherds for the Fulfillment Hour Administration.

(4) Collect information from the Shepherds for the Fulfillment Hour Administration.

(5) Identify any problems on Sunday mornings and report them to the Fulfillment Hour Administration.

(6) Be prepared to assist in resolving unexpected problems, when needed.

DEPARTMENT DIRECTOR
Preschool Division

The Department Director in the Preschool Division helps the Shepherds manage the learning activities and administrative duties whenever there are two or more Shepherds meeting in one room with a group of preschoolers.

Duties

(1) Assist the Shepherds and workers in all work of the department including Weekly Workers' Meeting, planning and evaluation.

(2) Greet the preschoolers when they enter the room.

(3) Direct the preschoolers to their appropriate areas.

(4) Collect the weekly Attendance Records and return them to the Fulfillment Hour office.

(5) Teach a small group of preschoolers during Bible study time, when needed.

(6) Help maintain department records—attendance, commitment forms for workers, class lists, etc.

(7) Be prepared and arrive on time.

APPENDIX 3 (cont'd)

(8) Discover and enroll new learners.

(9) Assist the Shepherds in contacting absentees as well as regular attendees.

(10) Minister, witness and fellowship with workers, preschoolers and their families.

(11) Assist the Shepherds in recording changes, drops and transfers.

(12) Assist the Shepherds in fulfilling the functions of Evangelism/Outreach, Discipleship, Fellowship, Ministry/Mission, Prayer and Care Group Leader.

DEPARTMENT DIRECTOR
Children's Division

The Department Director in the Children's Division helps the Shepherds manage the learning activities and administrative duties whenever there are two or more units within the same grade level.

<u>Duties</u>

(1) Assist the Shepherds and workers in all work of the department including Weekly Workers' Meeting, planning and evaluation.

(2) Direct the children to their appropriate classrooms.

(3) Assist the Shepherd with learning activities, when needed.

(4) Collect the weekly Attendance Records and return them to the Fulfillment Hour office.

(5) Act as a substitute Shepherd, when needed.

(6) Help maintain the department's records—attendance, commitment forms for workers, class lists, etc.

(7) Be prepared and arrive on time.

APPENDIX 3 (cont'd)

(8) Discover and enroll new learners.

(9) Assist the Shepherds in contacting absentees as well as regular attendees.

(10) Minister, witness and fellowship with workers, youth and their families.

(11) Assist the Shepherds in recording changes, drops and transfers.

(12) Assist the Shepherds in fulfilling the functions of Evangelism/Outreach, Discipleship, Fellowship, Ministry/Mission, Prayer and Care Group Leader.

DEPARTMENT DIRECTOR
Youth Division

The Department Director in the Youth Division helps the Shepherds manage the learning activities and administrative duties whenever there are two or more classes within the same grade level.

<u>Duties</u>

(1) Assist the Shepherds and workers in all work of the department including Weekly Workers' Meeting, planning and evaluation.

(2) Direct the youth to their appropriate classrooms.

(3) Assist the Shepherd with learning activities, when needed.

(4) Collect the weekly Attendance Records and return them to the Fulfillment Hour office.

(5) Act as a substitute Shepherd, when needed.

(6) Help maintain the department's records—attendance, commitment forms for workers, class lists, etc.

(7) Be prepared and arrive on time.

APPENDIX 3 (cont'd)

(8) Discover and enroll new learners.

(9) Assist the Shepherds in contacting absentees as well as regular attendees.

(10) Minister, witness and fellowship with workers, youth and their families.

(11) Assist the Shepherds in recording changes, drops and transfers.

(12) Assist the Shepherds in fulfilling the functions of Evangelism/Outreach, Discipleship, Fellowship, Ministry/Mission, Prayer and Care Group Leader.

DIVISION/DEPARTMENT SECRETARY

The Division/Department Secretary helps to maintain Fulfillment Hour records at the division and/or department level.

Duties

(1) Compile and maintain class records for all Fulfillment Hour classes/units within the department/division.

(2) Summarize the weekly Attendance Records from each Fulfillment Hour class/unit in the division/department.

(3) Compile all reports and statistics for the division/department. These statistics include:

    a. Enrollment
    b. Classes/units
    c. Attendance (weekly)
    d. Contacts (weekly)
    e. People with whom Christ was shared
    f. People accepting Christ
    g. Baptisms
    h. Guests
    i. Weekly Workers' Meeting Attendance
    j. Potential Workers' Training Graduates

(4) Maintain a list of workers in all positions within the division/department.

APPENDIX 3 (cont'd)

> # SHEPHERD

The Fulfillment Hour Shepherd directs all class activities. The Shepherd is responsible for everything that does or does not occur in the class. The Shepherd works with the Fulfillment Hour Division/Department Leaders to lead and manage the class/unit.

Duties

(1) Encourage and motivate each class learner to mature spiritually and be transformed into the likeness of Jesus Christ.

(2) Provide a quality learning experience for the class according to the assigned curriculum and the guidelines taught in the Potential Workers' Training module entitled "Modeling the Process of Teaching."

(3) Be theologically sound.

(4) Organize the class according to the standard Fulfillment Hour Class Organizational Chart. Enlist, encourage and motivate class leaders in the following positions: Missions Leader, Care Group Leaders, Secretary, Ministry Project Leader, Fellowship Leader, Evangelism/Outreach Leader, Discipleship Leader and Prayer Leader. *(Note: Shepherds in the Preschool and Children's Divisions perform these functions unless they are assigned to another adult worker.)*

(5) Keep an updated class organizational chart on file with the Fulfillment Hour Secretary, Coordinator/Director and the Department Director.

(6) Ensure all class position leaders complete the Potential Worker's Training.

(7) Perform the duties of all position leaders in the absence of an assigned leader.

(8) Maintain an updated class roll and report all changes to the Fulfillment Hour Secretary.

(9) Contact the class Care Group Leader(s) each week.

(10) Attend all Weekly Workers' Meetings.

(11) Lead the class to twin (reproduce) itself.

(12) Be a regular worshiper and tither.

(13) Advise the Fulfillment Hour Administration of all class activities.

APPENDIX 3 (cont'd)

CLASS SECRETARY

The Class Secretary works with the Fulfillment Hour Secretary to compile and maintain records for the Fulfillment Hour classes/units.

<u>Duties</u>

(1) Compile and maintain the class roster.

(2) Ensure that every member completes an enrollment record.

(3) Assist the Shepherd in maintaining a current organizational chart for the class.

(4) Prepare the weekly Attendance Record, making sure all fields are completed.

(5) Compile and maintain a class prospect list.

(6) Prepare and mail correspondence as requested by the class.

(7) Participate in the Fulfillment Hour Weekly Workers' Meetings.

(8) Share Fulfillment Hour administrative correspondence with the class.

(9) Submit record corrections to the Shepherd for approval.

(10) Maintain a record of all class activities.

APPENDIX 3 (cont'd)

PRAYER LEADER

The Fulfillment Hour Prayer Leader works with the church's Prayer Ministry to lead Fulfillment Hour class members to pray regularly. We believe that prayer must undergird the work of the church and will yield great power as we fulfill God's will for our lives.

<u>Duties</u>

(1) Lead the class in praying daily for the needs of class members, prospects and the church.

(2) Lead the class in giving praise reports and testimonies.

(3) Model how to conduct devotions in class fellowships and at home.

(4) Lead the class to participate in church-wide prayer activities.

(5) Participate in the Fulfillment Hour Weekly Workers' Meetings.

FELLOWSHIP LEADER

The Fulfillment Hour Fellowship Leader leads the class members in developing meaningful and nurturing relationships.

<u>Duties</u>

(1) Plan and coordinate fellowship activities that are designed to facilitate good personal relationships within the class.

(2) Assist the Shepherd in assimilating new members into the class.

(3) Lead the class in participating in at least one fellowship activity each month.

(4) Lead the class in participating in church-wide fellowship activities.

(5) Develop and implement class fellowship goals.

(6) Participate in the Fulfillment Hour Weekly Workers' Meetings.

APPENDIX 3 (cont'd)

MISSIONS LEADER

The Fulfillment Hour Missions Leader involves the class members in ministering to the needs of people who are outside of the church through various local, national and international mission projects.

Duties

(1) Plan and coordinate missions activities for the class.

(2) Build awareness among class members of local, national, and international mission needs through study, support and participation in projects.

(3) Lead the class in selecting mission projects to support and complete.

(4) Encourage the class to give regularly to church-wide missions activities.

(5) Encourage and lead the class in prayer for international, domestic and local missions, and all missionaries.

(6) Encourage the class members to develop a *missions lifestyle*.

(7) Participate in the Fulfillment Hour Weekly Workers' Meetings.

MINISTRY PROJECT LEADER

The Fulfillment Hour Ministry Project Leader involves the class members in ministering to the needs of members of the local church.

<u>Duties</u>

(1) Plan and coordinate class ministry activities.

(2) Keep the class aware of ministry needs of the class members and congregation.

(3) Lead the class in selecting ministry activities to support and complete.

(4) Encourage the class to support church-wide ministry activities.

(5) Identify and seek ways to meet special needs of members and prospects who are homebound or away from home.

(6) Develop and implement class ministry goals.

(7) Participate in the Fulfillment Hour Weekly Workers' Meetings.

APPENDIX 3 (cont'd)

> # DISCIPLESHIP LEADER

The Fulfillment Hour Discipleship Leader assists the Shepherd in developing disciples by encouraging class members in their personal Christian walk and involving them in discipleship training.

<u>Duties</u>

(1) Keep all class members aware of the need and opportunities for discipleship training.

(2) Encourage class members to regularly attend Bible Study and other discipleship training as a class or individually.

(3) Assist the Shepherd in providing training opportunities for class members.

(4) Work with the Shepherd and Minister of Discipleship to develop and implement discipleship training goals for the class.

(5) Work with the Shepherd to assess the class' spiritual growth needs annually.

(6) Encourage class members to take spiritual gifts training and employ their gifts in the ministries of the church.

(7) Encourage members to grow in their daily Christian walk through personal prayer, Bible study and devotion.

(8) Encourage members to attend evangelism training and become actively involved in witnessing and discipling others.

(9) Seek to mature in his/her personal relationship with God and be transformed into the likeness of Christ.

(10) Participate in the Fulfillment Hour Weekly Workers' Meetings.

APPENDIX 3 (cont'd)

EVANGELISM/OUTREACH LEADER

The Fulfillment Hour Evangelism/Outreach Leader leads the class members in sharing their faith and actively seeking to reach the lost.

<u>Duties</u>

(1) Plan and coordinate class outreach and visitation activities for the class.

(2) Lead the class in making weekly contacts.

(3) Assist the class' Discipleship Leader in encouraging the class to participate in evangelism training.

(4) Lead the class to participate in church-wide outreach efforts.

(5) Work with the Minister of Evangelism to develop and implement evangelism, visitation and outreach goals for the class.

(6) Participate in the Fulfillment Hour Weekly Workers' Meetings.

CARE GROUP LEADER

The Fulfillment Hour Care Group Leader helps the Shepherd and the Ministry Project Leader minister to the needs of class members.

Duties

(1) Visit or contact every member on a regular basis, being alert to needs that are expressed or observed.

(2) Report all ministry needs to the Shepherd.

(3) Perform ministry actions for class members.

(4) Work with the Ministry Project Leader in selecting ministry activities for the class.

(5) Witness to unsaved class members and lead un-churched Christian members to unite with the church.

(6) Encourage individual spiritual growth and participation in the Fulfillment Hour class.

(7) Report all ministry needs to the Shepherd.

APPENDIX 3 (cont'd)

(8) Assist the Shepherd with Fellowship and/or Prayer Leader responsibilities if no one is assigned to perform those functions.

(9) Participate in the Fulfillment Hour Weekly Workers' Meetings.

MEMBER

We feel honored to have individuals serving as members in our Fulfillment Hour classes. The expectations of members are as follows:

(1) Be willing to listen.

(2) Be willing to share.

(3) Be willing to participate.

(4) Be open to the Holy Spirit.

APPENDIX 4

SAMPLE FULFILLMENT HOUR
LEADERSHIP REQUIREMENTS CHECKLIST

Name _____ **Class** _____

___ Regular Fulfillment Hour Class Attendance
___ Regular Weekly Workers' Meeting Attendance
___ Sunday School Week   Date _____
___ Ministry Fest (GCBC)   Date _____
___ Potential Workers' Training   Date _____
___ Seven (7) Laws of the Learner   Date _____
___ Network Spiritual Gifts   Date _____
___ Growing Up to the Head   Date _____
___ Baptist Faith and Message   Date _____
___ Interview with Executive Pastor   Date _____

Pastor's Signature   **Signed** _____

DIVISIONAL ORIENTATION

Coordinator/Director's Signature

___ Adult   _____   Date ____
___ Youth   _____   Date ____
___ Children   _____   Date ____
___ Preschool   _____   Date ____

SAMPLE FULFILLMENT HOUR WORKER PROFILE

_____ Church

Name _____ Nickname_____

Address _____

Telephone # _____ E-mail _____

Occupation _____ How long?_____

Birthplace _____ How long in state?_____

High School/College name and location: _____

_____

Family Information (general): _____

_____

Hobbies _____

Something not generally known about you: _____

_____

How long as church member? _____

Activities at church:_____

_____

My Favorite _____ is _____

APPENDIX 6

SAMPLE SERVANT-LEADER FORM for PRESCHOOL, CHILDREN'S AND YOUTH WORKERS

This form is to be completed by all applicants for any position involving the supervision or custody of minors. It will help our church family provide a safe and secure environment for all preschoolers, children and youth who participate in our ministries and use our facilities.

PERSONAL

Name _____SSN _____

Please list other names by which you have been known, for example, maiden name or previous married name: _____

Present Address _____

City _____ State _____ Zip Code _____

Day Phone ( ) _____ Evening Phone ( ) _____

Marital Status _____ Occupation _____

On what date would you be available to begin? _____

What is your minimum length of commitment? _____

Do you have a current driver's license? Yes/No ____ What state? _____

Please list your license number: _____

Have you ever been charged with, indicted for, or pled guilty to any offense involving a minor?

Yes/No ____ If yes, please provide ALL information concerning convictions within the past five years on a separate page.

Have you ever been charged with, indicted for or pled guilty to any felony offense?

Yes/No ____ If yes, please provide ALL information concerning convictions within the past five years on a separate page.

SAMPLE SERVANT-LEADER FORM (cont'd)

CHURCH ACTIVITY

When did you make your profession of faith in Christ? _____

When were you baptized? _____

Are you a member of our church? Yes/No _____ If no, where are you a member? _____For how long? _____

List the names and addresses of other churches you have attended regularly during the past five years:

_____

_____

List all previous church work involving preschoolers, children or youth:

Church Name	Address	Type of Work	Duties

List all previous non-church work involving preschoolers, children, or youth:

Organization	Address	Telephone #

List any gifts, callings, training, education or other factors that have prepared you for teaching preschoolers, children or youth:

_____

_____

APPENDIX 6 (cont'd)

SAMPLE SERVANT-LEADER FORM (cont'd)

REFERENCES

List personal references (excluding friends or relatives):

Name	Address	Telephone #

APPLICANT'S STATEMENT

The information contained in this application is correct to the best of my knowledge. I authorize references or churches listed in this application to provide information (including opinions) they may have regarding my character and fitness for working with preschoolers, children or youth. I release all such references from any liability for furnishing such evaluations, provided they do so in good faith and without malice. I waive any right I may have to inspect references provided on my behalf. I understand that a complete criminal background check will be conducted through local, state and federal law enforcement agencies. Any adverse findings could affect my eligibility for employment or service. Should my application be accepted, I agree to be bound by the bylaws and policies of this church and to refrain from unscriptural conduct in the performance of my services on behalf of the church. I further state that I have carefully read the foregoing release and know the content thereof. I sign this release as my own free act. This is a legally binding agreement, which I have read and understand.

Signature: _____ **Date:** _____

SAMPLE FULFILLMENT HOUR
LEADER'S COMMITMENT COVENANT

This commitment is made between you and God and no one else.

Believing that the privilege of guiding people in the Christian way of life is worthy of my best, I covenant, as a leader in the Fulfillment Hour of my church, to:

[ ]   Order my conduct in keeping with the principles of God and seek the help of the Holy Spirit, that I may be faithful and efficient in my work. (Ps. 119:133)

[ ]   Be regular and punctual in attendance; and in case of unavoidable absence, give notice thereof as far in advance as possible. (1 Cor. 4:2)

[ ]   Thoroughly prepare for the lesson and my other duties each week. (2 Tim. 2:15)

[ ]   Use the Bible with my group on Sunday morning, or other meeting times, and help them to understand and love it. (Ps. 119:16)

[ ]   Contribute my tithe to my church. (Mal. 3:10)

[ ]   Regularly attend the Weekly Workers' Meetings. (Heb. 10:24-25)

[ ]   Visit prospects frequently and make a special effort to contact absentees each week. (Acts 2:46)

[ ]   Complete one or more courses from the "Track Around the Forest." (2 Tim. 2:15)

APPENDIX 7 (cont'd)

[ ]   Cooperate wholeheartedly in the plans and activities of the church and school. (1 Cor. 3:9)

[ ]   Be loyal to the program of the church, striving to attend all worship services. (Heb. 10:25)

[ ]   Make witnessing a major endeavor. (Prov. 11:30)

[ ]   Seek to discover and meet the needs of those with whom I come into contact, especially fellow church members and prospects for my church. (Gal. 6:2)

[ ]   Pray regularly for the church, the Fulfillment Hour, the officers, the Shepherds, the learners and their homes. (1 Thess. 5:17)

[ ]   Apply the teachings of Christ in moral and social issues of my everyday life. (Jas. 1:22)

[ ]   With the help of God, do my utmost to keep this covenant. (Phil. 2:13)

After much prayer, I will serve in the position of _____ for one year.

_____   _____   _____
Date   **Fulfillment Hour Leader's Signature**   **Class/Div./Dept.**

ENLISTMENT IN ACTION

A skit written by Jackie S. Henderson

PART I

Narr:	It's High Attendance Sunday at the "Good Teaching is Our Motto" Baptist Church. Min. Johnson, the Minister/Director of Christian Education, has just arrived. As she looks around, she sees crowds of people coming to Fulfillment Hour— more than ever before. She suddenly remembers that Pastor asked her six months ago to enlist some new Fulfillment Hour Shepherds in preparation for High Attendance Sunday.
Min. of CE:	Oh no, Pastor asked me six months ago to get some new Shepherds for the Fulfillment Hour. I forgot all about it. What am I going to do? I know!...I am going to get some Shepherds...today..."by whatever means necessary."
Lady:	(Casually walking by)
Min. of CE:	Hey, you! Do you go to church here?
Lady:	No! I'm just visiting. I live in Moundstown, Georgia.
Min. of CE:	Oh, it doesn't matter. I need a Shepherd for the Adult Division Fulfillment Hour. I really need you to start in a few minutes.
Lady:	I know you don't mean me.
Min. of CE:	Why not? I'm sure you will do fine. Let me tell you where to find your class.

APPENDIX 8 (cont'd)

Lady: But...but...I live about an hour from here.

Min. of CE: Don't worry. The class will just have to wait on Sundays until you get there. That will just give them more time to finish gossiping about each other.

Lady: But...but...I don't know what to do...I don't know what to teach.

Min. of CE: I'm sure they have some books left in the room. People are always leaving books everywhere. Just get one and start teaching. You'll be fine. Go ahead now. (Points the way to the class) Whew! One down.

...   (Man appears, talking on cell phone)

Min. of CE: A man! I need a man!

Man: (Stops suddenly, starts smiling. Rubs his hair, massages his mustache.)

Min. of CE: Don't get too excited! It's NOT what you think. I need a male Shepherd for the preschool division.

Man: I'm no Shepherd!

Min. of CE: It's alright. It'll be fun. The class needs you...the little angels (grins under breath). The little angels need a big strong man like you.

Man: I'm not even a member of your church.

Min. of CE: But you are here NOW.

Man: I've never taught before.

Min. of CE: We all have to start at some point.

Man: But I don't even like children.

Min. of CE: No problem. They'll just grow on you.

Man: Ok. I'll give it a try. But I don't like children. They get on my nerves. Always asking questions...wanting to know things.

Min. of CE: Sh....We'll let that be our secret.

Man: But I don't like children.

Min. of CE: That's ok now. You just go right that way. Tell the children you are their new Shepherd.
                I knew I could do it! Enlisting is not that hard.

...

Teen: (Teen appears) Y'all hiring!

Min. of CE: You came to the right place!

Teen: I need a job. My dad said that if I want this car I saw at the dealership, I'm going to have to pay for it myself. I really need a job.

Min. of CE: Dad knows best. I can put you to work right away. Today even. In fact, right now.

Teen: What about the pay?

APPENDIX 8 (cont'd)

Min. of CE: The pay is not much, but the benefits are out of this world!

Teen: That sounds great! What will I have to do?

Min. of CE: Mostly...just talk.

Teen: Oh, I can surely handle that. My mom is always telling me I talk too much. I can't wait to tell her I got a job just talking.

Min. of CE: Go ahead now. You don't want to be late for your first day on the job. I'll tell Pastor that he had nothing to worry about. I enlisted three new Shepherds in a matter of minutes. I did it! I, I, I really did it!

Narr: Now that's one way of enlisting workers. However, not the right away.

PART II

Narr: Let's rewind the clock. It's High Attendance Sunday at the "Good Teaching is Our Motto" Baptist Church. The Minister/Director of Christian Education has just arrived. As she looks around, she sees crowds of people coming to Fulfillment Hour, more than ever before.

Min. of CE: (Smiling) I am so glad Pastor encouraged me six months ago to get some new Shepherds for the Fulfillment Hour. And organizing the Potential Workers' Class was a great idea. We had fifteen graduates last month. Today is High Attendance Sunday, and I am so glad we are ready to receive this big crowd of people today.

Narr: Let's look back to four months ago. We are finalizing our enlistment process. Min. Johnson, the Minister/Director of Christian Education, is interviewing prospective workers.

Sis. Cobb: (Enters the room) Min. Johnson, I am here for our meeting.

Min. of CE: Sis. Cobb, thank you so much for agreeing to meet with me. Come in and have a seat. As I mentioned to you on the phone last week, I asked you to pray over becoming a Fulfillment Hour Shepherd in the Adult Division. Did you do that?

Sis. Cobb: Oh yes, I did!

Min. of CE: I have been reviewing your ministry activities since you have been a member of our church and your attendance at worship and at Fulfillment Hour. In fact, I have glowing recommendations from your Fulfillment Hour Shepherd.

Sis. Cobb: Thanks so very much. This church is very thorough in its enlistment process.

Min. of CE: Yes, we have to be. This is God's church, and we want to give Him the very best. Here is the Shepherd position description so we can discuss what is expected. We also have an eight-week Potential Workers' Training class that we want you to attend. Now, don't think you will be left alone after you start teaching. We believe in ongoing training. After all, there is no such thing as a trained worker, only workers in training.

APPENDIX 8 (cont'd)

Sis. Cobb: Thank you so much for this opportunity to teach in the Adult Division. I won't let you down. I won't let God down.

...

Bro. Smith: Good morning, Min. Johnson.

Min. of CE: Good morning. Thanks for coming. Have a seat. I have reviewed your resume and your criminal background report. We spoke to your references and some neighbors.

Bro. Smith: Yes, I understand the need to be thorough in checking backgrounds, especially when working with kids.

Min. of CE: This is true. However, everything checks out fine. We look forward to working with you in the Preschool Division. Go two doors down the hall and the Preschool Director is waiting to show you around and answer any other questions you may have. Again, thank you for accepting God's call to work with His children.

Min. of CE: Sis. Brown, please come in and have a seat.

Sis. Brown: Hello, again. I am very impressed with the Youth Division. Thanks for sending me on the tour, as well as letting me sit in during the Weekly Workers' Meeting.

Min. of CE: We are very happy to have you work in our Fulfillment Hour. Your eagerness to serve stood out even in Potential Workers' Training. However, because your experience in Fulfillment Hour work is very limited, we would like for you to start by working in the Youth Division as Secretary.

Sis. Brown: Oh, that will be fine!

Min. of CE: This will give you the opportunity to observe up close what happens each Sunday morning. You will work closely with the Shepherd who will serve as your mentor for six months. Afterward, we will look toward promoting you to Shepherd in your own class.

Sis. Brown: Thanks so much. I am a quick learner. You just wait and see. I will do my very best.

Min. of CE: I am sure you will. Thanks for coming.

Narr: A successful Fulfillment Hour is definitely linked to good, positive enlistment of qualified workers—workers who feel "called" to do God's ministry in Fulfillment Hour.

APPENDIX 9

SAMPLE FULFILLMENT HOUR ANNUAL BUDGET

Item	No. Items	Unit Cost	Quarterly Total
QUARTERLY MATERIALS			
Adult - Learner	1550	$ 1.50	$ 2,325.00
Adult - Leader	150	4.00	600.00
Adult - Leader's Pack	10	13.00	130.00
Adv. Bible Study Commentary (NIV)	50	3.50	175.00
Hershel Hobbs Commentary (KJV)	100	4.60	460.00
Youth - Learner	462	1.50	2,772.00
Youth - Leader	34	4.00	693.00
Youth - Leader's Packs w/CD	33	16.00	528.00
Children - Learner	273	1.60	436.80
Children - Leader	40	4.00	160.00
Children - Leader's Packs	30	17.50	525.00
Children - Teaching Pictures	30	7.80	234.00
Children - Memory Verses	3	1.00	3.00
Preschool - Learner's Guide	138	1.50	207.00
Preschool - Leader's Pack	7	19.00	133.00
Preschool - Leader's Guide	32	4.00	128.00
Preschool - Music CD	4	10.95	43.80
Preschool - Floor Puzzles	4	14.99	59.96
Nursery - Learner's Guide	15	1.50	22.50
Nursery - Leader's Pack	5	19.95	99.75
Nursery - Music for Babies	4	10.95	175.20
Deaf (FBS Adult Learner - KJV Lg. Print)	12	1.50	43.80
Deaf (FBS Adult Leader - KJV)	4	4.00	16.00
Deaf (EBS Adult Leader Guide)	1	4.00	4.00
Deaf (EBS for Deaf Students)	3	2.70	8.10

SAMPLE FULFILLMENT HOUR ANNUAL BUDGET

Item	No. Items	Unit Cost	Quarterly Total
Wed. Noon - Adult Learner Guide	50	$ 1.50	$ 300.00
Wed. Noon - Adult Leader Guide	2	4.00	32.00
Wed. Noon - Adult Leader Pack	1	13.00	52.00
TOTAL QUARTERLY MATERIALS			7,285.71
SHIPPING & HANDLING			2,500.00
TOTAL QUARTERLY MATERIAL COST			9,785.71
TOTAL ANNUAL MATERIALS COST			$ 39,142.84

Item	No. Items	Unit Cost	Annual Total
SUPPLIES			
Posters, Certificates, Paper Products			$ 700.00
Postcards	4000		600.00
Enrollment Cards	5000		460.00
Collection Envelopes	1000		50.00
Easel Pads	100	10.00	1,000.00
White Board Pens/Erasers			125.00
FH Office Supplies			447.00
Other			
TOTAL SUPPLIES			3,732.00
TRAINING			
Sunday School Week – Ridgecrest, NC	30	200.00	6,000.00
Black Church Week – Ridgecrest, NC	30	200.00	6,000.00
Regional Training			1,900.00
Local Training (2-day)	20	40.00	800.00
Local Training (1-day)	30	5.00	150.00
Preparation Day			2,000.00
TOTAL TRAINING			$ 16,850.00

APPENDIX 9 (cont'd)

SAMPLE FULFILLMENT HOUR ANNUAL BUDGET

Item	No. Items	Unit Cost	Annual Total
MINISTRY ACTIVITIES			
Easter Egg Hunt			$ 474.00
Annual Appreciation Banquet			2,000.00
Harvest Festival			1,100.00
Special Events			1,000.00
Miscellaneous			500.00
TOTAL MINISTRY ACTIVITIES			$ 5,074.00
DIVISION BUDGETS			
Preschool Division			1,000.00
Children's Division			1,300.00
Youth Division			1,300.00
Adult Division			2,300.00
TOTAL DIVISION BUDGETS			$ 5,900.00
OTHER			
Mailings to All Workers (~400)			
Postcards			800.00
Postage			900.00
The FH Care Plus Team			
Cards (Get Well, Sympathy, etc.)			800.00
Postage			500.00
TOTAL OTHER			$ 3,000.00
TOTAL ANNUAL FH REQUEST			$ 73,698.84

SAMPLE CALENDAR OF EVENTS
CHRISTIAN EDUCATION & FULFILLMENT HOUR MINISTRY

Jan. 5	FH Preparation Day: Book Study with Pastor (10:00 a.m. - 12:00 noon.)
Jan. 19	ALL SAINTS WORKSHOP
Feb. 2	FH Preparation Day: Book Study with Pastor (10:00 a.m. - 12 noon)
Feb. 6–Mar. 13	FH Potential Workers class
Mar 10	FH High Attendance Sunday
Mar 20	FH Seven Laws of the Learner (Rooms 1/3)
Mar 31	FH Resurrection Day Assembly (9:30 am)
April 6	FH Preparation Day: Book Study with Pastor (10:00 a.m. - 12 noon)
April	Annie Armstrong Easter Offering
May 4	FH Preparation Day: Book Study with Pastor (10:00 am - 12 noon)
May 12	Women's Day – Female Shepherd Day
June	Support for International Missions & Evangelism Month
June 1	FH Preparation Day: Book Study with Pastor (10:00 a.m. - 12 noon)
June 9	FH High Attendance Sunday
June 3-7	Vacation Bible School
June 16	Men's Day - Male Teachers for Youth/Adults; Male presence for Children/Preschool
July	Support for International Missions Trip & World Changers
July 14-18	Revival
July 15-19	Ministry Fest

APPENDIX 10 (cont'd)

SAMPLE CALENDAR OF EVENTS
CHRISTIAN EDUCATION & FULFILLMENT HOUR MINISTRY

July 22-26	Sunday School Leadership Training
Aug.	Mission Project (School items for back-to-school)
Aug. 3	FH Preparation Day: Book Study with Pastor (10:00 a.m. - 12 noon)
Sep.	Individual Class Mission/Ministry Project
Sep. 4-Oct. 9	Potential Workers' Training
Sep. 15	Pastor's Anniversary
Sep. 15	FH High Attendance Sunday
Sep. 28	Teachers' Workshop (Discipleship Ministry)
Oct.	North American Mission Board Project – TBA
Oct. 5	FH Preparation Day: Book Study with Pastor (10:00 a.m. - 12 noon)
Oct. 13	World Hunger Sunday
Oct. 31	FH Harvest Time Festival, Fellowship Hall (7:00 p.m. – 8:30 p.m.)
Nov.	Encourage class members to sign Commitment Cards
Nov. 3	FH Annual Appreciation Banquet
Nov.	Thanksgiving Baskets (Mission Project for Assigned Classes)
Dec. 1-8	Week of Prayer/Mission Study for Int'l Missions & Lottie Moon Christmas Offering
Dec.	Christmas Baskets (Mission Project) for Assigned Classes
Dec. 22	FH Hour Christmas Program Assembly

MEETING SPACE SPECIFICATIONS CHART

Taken from *Sunday School for a New Century* by Taylor & Hank © 1999

Age Group	Space/ Person	Maximum Attendance	Room Size	Leader-Learner Ratio
Preschool				
Babies	35 sq. ft.	12	420 sq. ft.	1:2
Ones– Twos	35 sq. ft.	12	420 sq. ft.	1:3
Threes– Pre-K	35 sq. ft.	16	560 sq. ft.	1:4
Kinder- garten	35 sq. ft.	20	700 sq. ft.	1:5
Children				
Grades 1–6	20-25 sq. ft.	24	480–600 sq. ft.	1:6
Youth				
Grades 7–12 (Class)	10–12 sq. ft.	12	120–144 sq. ft.	1:12
Grades 7–12 (Dept.)	8–10 sq. ft.	65	520–650 sq. ft.	
Young Adults (18–24 yrs.)				
Dept.	10 sq. ft.			1:4
Class	12 sq. ft.	25	300 sq. ft.	
Dual Use	15–18 sq. ft.	25	375–450 sq. ft.	
Adults (25 yrs. & up)				
Dept.	10 sq. ft.			1:4
Class	12 sq. ft.	25	300 sq. ft.	
Dual Use	15–18 sq. ft.	25	375–450 sq. ft.	

APPENDIX 12

SAMPLE JOSHUA MINISTRY TRIBES

TRIBE OF EPHRAIM		TRIBE OF MANASSEH	
Tribal Leader:		**Tribal Leader:**	
Genesis 2	Illuminators	Amazing Grace	The Redeemed
Doorkeepers	Young Marrieds	Charity	Coming of Age
Messengers	Upward Bound	Disciples for Christ	Pastor's New Members Class
Renewed Spirit	Victory	The Abiders	New Warriors
Young Adults I	Logos	Faithful Followers	New Creations
Adult II	By Grace	Meditations	Outreachers
Discipleship		Men's Bible Fellowship	Titus
		Upper Room	

TRIBE OF REUBEN		TRIBE OF GAD	
Tribal Leader:		**Tribal Leader:**	
Adult I	New Beginning	Blessed Assurance	Trailblazers
Adult III	Unspeakable Joy	Good News	New Song of Solomon
Adult IV	Truth Seekers	Life Changers	Virtuous Women
Bible Explorers	Young Adults II	Light Bearers	Young Adult III
Loyal Bereans	Genesis I	Married in Christ	Seekers of the Word
Millennium	The Branches	Samuel	Christian Pioneers
The Pentecostals	The Innkeepers	Temple of the Holy Spirit	Young Adults IV
Word Warriors	Life in the Word		

SAMPLE FULFILLMENT HOUR FELLOWSHIP ACTIVITIES

PRESCHOOL

(1) Hayride, caroling, skating, bowling, sports, movies
(2) Activities for students and Shepherds
(3) Activities for adult workers only
(4) Open house to include parents, Shepherds, guests and prospects

CHILDREN

(1) Drama, Bible study or musical
(2) Parties, cookouts, field days, Harvest Festival, jamboree, carnival or, games
(3) Friends' social
(4) Parent and child fellowship

YOUTH

(1) W.O.W.—Worship on Wednesday
(2) Cookout
(3) Bowling or skating
(4) Sports activity
(5) Movies

APPENDIX 13 (cont'd)

SAMPLE FULFILLMENT HOUR FELLOWSHIP ACTIVITIES

ADULTS

(1) Class breakfast to welcome new members
(2) Fellowship meal (breakfast, lunch or dinner)
(3) Department picnic
(4) Bowling
(5) Theatre/movie
(6) Shower (wedding, baby, anniversary, etc.)
(7) Sports activity (baseball, basketball, golf, tennis, etc.)
(8) Thanksgiving/Christmas gathering
(9) Valentine fellowship with homebound members
(10) Christmas caroling
(11) Potluck dinner
(12) Nursing home visitations

APPENDIX 14

SAMPLE FELLOWSHIP MENU SIGN-UP SHEET

Item	Quantity	Name	Phone
MEATS			
Chicken	_____	_____	_____
Ham	_____	_____	_____
Turkey	_____	_____	_____
VEGETABLES			
Greens	_____	_____	_____
Beans	_____	_____	_____
Macaroni & Cheese	_____	_____	_____
Casserole	_____	_____	_____
Potatoes	_____	_____	_____
SALADS			
Green	_____	_____	_____
Potato	_____	_____	_____
DESSERTS			
Cake	_____	_____	_____
Pie	_____	_____	_____
BREADS			
Rolls	_____	_____	_____
Cornbread	_____	_____	_____

APPENDIX 14 (cont'd)

SAMPLE FELLOWSHIP MENU SIGN-UP SHEET

Item	Quantity	Name	Phone
DRINKS			
Soft Drinks	_____	_____	_____
Tea	_____	_____	_____
OTHER			
Plates	_____	_____	_____
Cups	_____	_____	_____
Napkins	_____	_____	_____
Forks/Spoons/			
Knives	_____	_____	_____
Ice	_____	_____	_____

SAMPLE ATTENDANCE RECORD

Fulfillment Hour Class Roster

_____ **Church**

Report Date _____

Division: _____ **Department:** _____

Class: _____

"P" = Present	Name	Position	# Contacts	Shared Christ	Received Christ
[ ]	Student A	Member	[ ]	[ ]	[ ]
[ ]	Student B	Member	[ ]	[ ]	[ ]
[ ]	Student C	Member	[ ]	[ ]	[ ]
[ ]	Student D	Member	[ ]	[ ]	[ ]
[ ]	Student E	Prayer Leader	[ ]	[ ]	[ ]
[ ]	Shepherd	Shepherd	[ ]	[ ]	[ ]

Total Members Present _____   **Total # Contacts** _____

Total Guests Present _____   **Total # Shared Christ** _____

TOTAL PRESENT _____   **Total # Received Christ** _____

Today's Shepherd: _____

Guests: _____   _____

                _____   _____

                _____   _____

PLEASE RETURN ATTENDANCE RECORD
TO THE FH OFFICE EACH SUNDAY.

APPENDIX 16

SAMPLE FULFILLMENT HOUR GOALS for 2003

Setting a goal is not the main thing, it is "the plans I have for you declares the Lord, plans to prosper you and not harm you, plans to give you hope and a future." Jeremiah 29:11 (NIV)

(1) **DIVISIONAL GROWTH:** Start a Young Adult Division that consists of 10 Classes.

(2) **IN-HOUSE TRAINING:** Conduct two Potential Workers' Training Courses (February-March and August-October).

(3) **ENLISTMENT:** Enlist 40 new Shepherds.

(4) **LEADERSHIP:** 100% re-commitment of all workers in the 2003 stewardship ministry program.

(5) **ENROLLMENT:** Enroll 500 new members.

(6) **TWINNING**: Enlist 25 Apprentices for 25 Adult FH Classes in accordance to the same procedures as used for enlisting Shepherds.

(7) **ASSOCIATIONAL/STATE TRAINING:** Send 50 FH workers to state training seminars.

(8) **UNIT GROWTH:** Start 40 new units by the Pastor's anniversary on September 15, 2002.

(9) **EVANGELISM:** Have every class represented in the church's witnessing ministry for 100% participation.

(10) **BUDGET:** Monitor all spending to assure that Fulfillment Hour stays within the allotted budget.

The above goals will enable Fulfillment Hour to fulfill God's purposes of the church through **EVANGELISM**, **DISCIPLESHIP**, **FELLOWSHIP**, **MINISTRY** and **WORSHIP**.

APPENDIX 17

SAMPLE POTENTIAL WORKERS' TRAINING COURSE OUTLINE

_____ **Church**

Classes Held on Wednesdays, 7:00 - 8:30 p.m.

"And thou shalt love the Lord thy God . . ." Deut. 6:5a
"And thou shall teach them diligently . . ." Deut. 6:7a

<u>1ST QTR.</u>	<u>TRAINING/COURSE OVERVIEW</u>	<u>INSTRUCTOR</u>
Feb. 6	Orientation to Fulfillment Hour Registration - Expectations	_____
Feb. 13	Modeling the Process of Teaching GOSS (Growth-Oriented Sunday School)	_____
Feb. 16	Soul-Winning Training & Blitz	_____
Feb. 20	Fulfilling the Purposes of the Church	_____
Feb. 27	Age Level I Training - Preschool, Children's, Youth and Adults	_____
Feb. 27	Visit Weekly Workers' Meeting (6:15 p.m.) Serve as Prayer Leader (6:15 - 6:35 p.m.) Secretary's Training	_____
Mar. 2	Discipleship Training	_____
Mar. 6	Age Level II Training - Preschool, Children's, Youth Traits of Effective Teaching (Adults)	_____
Mar. 13	Wrap Up: The Complete Fulfillment Hour Picture & Fellowship	_____

100% ATTENDANCE REQUIREMENT FOR CERTIFICATION

GREENFOREST COMMUNITY BAPTIST CHURCH FULFILLMENT HOUR (SUNDAY SCHOOL) LEADERSHIP MEETINGS

by Sis. Joan W. Johnson
(Article reprinted from *Leadership Magazine*, January 2002)

Sunday School leadership meetings are known as Weekly Workers' Meetings at Greenforest. This is a time of celebration, inspiration, information, relationship building, missions and excitement.

In the earlier years, the eighties, our Pastor, Dr. George O. McCalep Jr., led all of our workers' meetings twice a month for children and preschool workers together, and adults and youth workers together. The writer had just become superintendent and knew very little about how a Sunday School should be set up or run. We received help from the Atlanta Baptist Association as it related to Sunday School training. For this training, we thank God.

It was during these times that we were introduced to the Growth Spiral and the Nine Basics for Good Sunday School. We practice these principles. Our Pastor believed in all of these principles. However, Weekly Workers' Meetings, now Leadership Meetings, were given priority on the calendar. No other meetings are scheduled during this time. We started having meetings weekly. Leaders on all levels are empowered. Our Pastor is supportive with his presence. However, Fulfillment Hour (Sunday School) is the ministry of the laity. Therefore, when the Pastor presents to the workers, "it is an impending event."

Leadership meetings begin in an environmental setting with music and a sense of excitement in the air. Based on Fulfillment Hour (Sunday School) Class locations, tables and chairs are placed in four tribes: Tribe of Ephraim, Tribe of Gad, Tribe of Manasseh and Tribe of Reuben. These tribes represent the army of God. Two tables are at the entrance—one with agendas,

APPENDIX 18 (cont'd)

announcements and adult lesson plans; the second table with the Prospects of the Week (POWs). When workers arrive, they sit in their assigned tribal area. All workers meet together for the first thirty minutes.

Each Wednesday at 6:15 p.m., Fulfillment Hour Leadership Meetings begin with devotion and prayer led by Prayer Leaders from the Adult Division. From 6:30 - 6:40 p.m., we have community and relationship building time. This is a time for leaders to get to know each other. All workers attend Weekly Leadership Meetings: Shepherds (name for teachers), Outreach/ Evangelism Leader, Prayer Leaders, Discipleship Leaders, Ministry/Missions Project Leaders, Secretaries, Fellowship Leaders and Care Group Leaders. At 6:45 p.m., divisional breakout takes place. Each division conducts planning and Bible study.

There is no general assembly of all workers on the first Wednesday. We have positional breakouts for every position. The youth, children's and pre-school workers meet for an hour instead of forty minutes. Specialized training is provided for each ministry position.

We celebrate the members' birthdays, promote church functions (such as High Attendance Sundays), praise reports and Jesus' birthday. The leaders are inspired to continue to come. They are often told that "they are not only good, but the best... even better than they think they are." Why do they continue to come to Workers' Meetings? It's because their commitment is to God and no one else. "And whatsoever you do, do it heartily, as to the Lord and not to men" (Col. 3:23).

It is a favor from God for me to be a part of the Greenforest Community Baptist Church Fulfillment Hour. Fulfillment Hour is the infrastructure and delivery system in our church. We lead people to a faith in our Lord and Savior Jesus Christ and build Great Commission Christians through small group Bible study classes that are involved in all of the purposes of God: Evangelism, Discipleship, Fellowship, Ministry and Worship. I thank the Lord for our Pastor, Dr. George O. McCalep, Jr., for giving me the privilege to serve God through the Sunday School.

SAMPLE FULFILLMENT HOUR
CLASS/SHEPHERD OBSERVATION FORM

(1) I observed this Department/Class on _____.

(2) The number of learners in attendance was _____.

(3) The teaching time was organized as follows:

_____   _____

_____   _____

_____   _____

(4) The Shepherd modeled the Fulfillment Hour process by:

(5) The following learning aids were used:

(6) The Bible was used in these ways:

(7) The thing that impressed me most was:

APPENDIX 19 (cont'd)

(8) I would suggest the following for improvement:

(9) Comments or additional observations

Signed _____ Date _____

SAMPLE FLIER

FULFILLMENT HOUR
"HIGH ATTENDANCE DAY"

on

PASTOR'S ANNIVERSARY

My Gift to Pastor is

MY ATTENDANCE at Fulfillment Hour

_____ *Church*

Sunday, September 16, XXXX

9:45 a.m. – 10:45 a.m.

APPENDIX 21

GOAL-REACHING AWARD

presented to

_____ *Class*

for Successfully Reaching 100%
of
Attendance & Contact Goals

_____ *Church*

"A goal untold is a defeatist attitude"
March 10, XXXX

_____ _____ _____
Superintendent   **Minister of**   **Pastor**
Christian Education

20th ANNUAL FULFILLMENT HOUR
2002 WORKERS' APPRECIATION BANQUET

"Fulfillment Hour: Our Role in Twinning God's Grace"
John 15:1-2

November 2, 2002
6:00 p.m.

Greenforest Community Baptist Church
3250 Rainbow Drive
Decatur, Georgia 30034

Sis. Jackie Henderson, Superintendent
Dea. Edward Henderson, Asst. Superintendent
Sis. Joan Johnson, Minister/Director of Christian Education

Rev. George O. McCalep Jr., Pastor

APPENDIX 22 (cont'd)

20th ANNUAL FULFILLMENT HOUR
2002 WORKERS' APPRECIATION BANQUET

Master & Mistress of Ceremonies

PROGRAMME

Devotion . . . . .Prayer Leaders

Welcome . . . . ._____

Opening Prayer . . . . ._____

Musical Presentation . . . . ._____

Occasion . . . . ._____

Potential Worker Graduate Presentations . . . . ._____

Blessing . . . . ._____

DINNER

Musical Presentation . . . . _____

Challenge to FH Workers . . . . _____

2001 Shepherd of the Year (keynote address) . . . . _____
_____*Class*

Evangelism Award . . . . _____

Distinguished Awards . . . . _____

Closing Remarks & Benediction . . . . _____

FULFILLMENT HOUR DISTINGUISHED AWARDS

Shepherd of the Year Award

Presented to the Fulfillment Hour Shepherd who, in the opinion of the Pastor and the Fulfillment Hour Administration, has provided spiritual nourishment, care and nurturing for his/her Fulfillment Hour class/unit as a whole, as well as each individual in the class/unit. This Shepherd comes to class prepared, regularly attends FH training sessions, encourages individual and classroom growth, promotes FH activities, prays regularly for and with his/her students, constantly seeks and trains new workers, actively supports the mission of the church, seeks to lead unsaved persons to Christ, and serves as an example of Christian living and stewardship to the members of his/her class/unit and to others. The Shepherd of the Year shares the vision of the church. This Shepherd acknowledges and executes his/her role in fulfilling the purposes of God through Fulfillment Hour.

Servantship Award

Presented to the Fulfillment Hour worker who, in the opinion of the Pastor and the Fulfillment Hour Administration, has demonstrated the willingness to voluntarily serve without reservation; who has prayerfully supported the Fulfillment Hour leadership and has diligently promoted the total Fulfillment Hour program.

APPENDIX 22 (cont'd)

Spirit Award

Presented to the Fulfillment Hour worker who, in the opinion of the Pastor and the Fulfillment Hour Administration, has consistently supported the total Fulfillment Hour program without reservation; who has discharged responsibility of his/her office with diligence; and who has demonstrated independent leadership while prayerfully carrying out the instructions of the Pastor, promoting cohesion and oneness of purpose, while continuing to display a Christ-like Spirit.

ABOUT THE AUTHORS

Joan W. Johnson has been a member of Greenforest Community Baptist Church for 22 years. She served as Sunday School Director from 1981-1986; Potential Worker Coordinator from 1987-1989; and as Class Planter from 1991-1997. Presently, she serves as Director of Christian Education. Under her leadership, Greenforest's Fulfillment Hour (Sunday School) enrollment has grown from 100 to over 5,000. As a result of her work at the associational level (from 1986 to the present), numerous churches have requested her help with their Sunday Schools. Joan retired from the Atlanta Public Schools were she served as a school nurse for 24 years.

Jackie S. Henderson joined Greenforest Community Baptist Church in 1993. She immediately enrolled in a Fulfillment Hour class and has been active in Fulfillment Hour there every since. After six short months, she began serving as Substitute Shepherd (Teacher) in her class and six months later, became Adult Division Director. In 1997, she became Superintendent of Fulfillment Hour where she still serves today. Jackie is employed at Emory University as the Finance/Data Manager in the Department of Family and Preventive Medicine.

Other Resources by George O. McCalep, Jr., Ph.D.
Committed to Doing Church God's Way

ORDER FORM

QTY	ITEM	EACH	TOTAL
	Faithful Over a Few Things	19.95	
	Faithful Over a Few Things—Study Guide	9.95	
	Faithful Over a Few Things—Audio Version	14.95	
	Faithful Over a Few Things—Resource Kit	189.95	
	Breaking the Huddle	14.95	
	Breaking the Huddle—Sermonic Audiocassette	10.00	
	Growing Up to the Head	19.95	
	Growing Up to the Head—Leader's Guide	10.95	
	Growing Up to the Head—Participant's Guide	10.95	
	Stir Up the Gifts	24.95	
	Stir Up the Gifts—Leader's Guide	10.95	
	Stir Up the Gifts—Workbook & Study Guide	10.95	
	Stir Up the Gifts—Sermonic Audio Series	19.95	
	Praising the Hell Out of Yourself	19.95	
	Praising the Hell Out of Yourself—Workbook	14.95	
	Praising the Hell Out of Yourself—CD	14.95	
	Praising the Hell Out of Yourself—T-Shirt (L, XL, XXL, XXXL)	10.00	
	Sin in the House	19.95	
	How to Be Blessed	19.95	
	"Jabez's Prayer"—Sermonic Audio Series	19.95	
	A Good Black Samaritan	3.95	
	Messages of Victory for God's Church in the New MIllennium—Sermonic Audio Series	19.95	
	Tough Enough: Trials on Every Hand by Sadie T. McCalep, Ph.D.	20.00	
	Subtotal		

Order by phone, fax, mail or online

Orman Press
4200 Sandy Lake Drive
Lithonia, GA 30038
Phone: 770-808-0999
Fax: 770-808-1955

www.ormanpress.com

ITEM	AMOUNT
Subtotal	
Postage & Handling (Call for Shipping Charges)	
C.O.D. (Add $6 plus Postage & Handling)	
Total	

Date_____Name_____

Adress_____Apt./Unit_____

City_____State_____Zip_____

Credit Card #_____Exp. Date_____

Visit our web site @ www.ormanpress.com
Your one-stop store for Christian resources

Pastor and Sister McCalep are available to conduct
workshops and seminars on all of these resources.
Call 404-486-6740 for scheduling information.

THE EDITOR'S RECOMMENDATIONS

God has given me a burning passion for biblically based kingdom building and spiritual growth. Through His Spirit, I have discerned and recorded in my books discipleship principles related to church growth, evangelism, personal spiritual development, praise and worship. I recommend the following titles to those who are serious about *doing church God's way*.

Church Growth and Kingdom Building

Faithful Over a Few Things: Seven Critical Church Growth Principles bridges the gap between theory and practice. It offers seven prinicples that when faithfully implemented will cause your church to grow. The book is available in print and audio versions. A study guide and resource kit are also available. The resource kit contains a workbook, transparencies and a videotape.

Sin in the House: Ten Crucial Church Problems with Cleansing Solutions examines problems that hinder growth and offers proven solutions. This book addresses the question of why you and your church are not growing.

Evangelism

Breaking the Huddle contains twelve messages that deal with the central theme of fulfilling Jesus' purpose of seeking and saving the lost. (Luke 19:10) Like a football team, the church must break the huddle, that is, leave the comfort of the sanctuary and obediently go out among the unsaved to share the Gospel.

Personal Spiritual Development

Growing Up to the Head: Ten Essentials to Becoming a Better Christian challenges the reader to mature spiritually by growing up to the fullness of Christ. The study is based on the book of Ephesians. The book uniquely relates personal spiritual growth to numerical congregational growth. A new participant's guide and leader's guide are now available.

Stir Up the Gifts: Empowering Believers for Victorious Living and Ministry Tasks is a complete, practical guide on spiritual gifts that is applicable for any denomination. The book is based on 2 Timothy 1:6 where Paul tells us to stir up the gift and bring the fire to a flame. Study of this book will fire you up and revolutionize the ministries in your church. A leader's guide and study guide are available.

How to Be Blessed: Finding Favor with God and Man is a biblical guide to being blessed according to God's Word. It is based on the truth that God promises to bless His obedient children. This book will protect you from finding out too late about all the blessings that were yours, but you never received.

Praise and Worship

Although the title is colorful, ***Praising the Hell Out of Yourself*** is a beneficial discipleship approach to praise and worship. It offers praise as an antidote for evil and provides the "how, why and when" of entering into His presence. A workbook, CD and T-shirt are available.

Inspiration

My wife's autobiography, ***Tough Enough: Trials on Every Hand*** describes how God transformed a shy, reserved, country girl from Alabama into a bold, self-assured, yet humble helpmeet to her husband and spokesperson for the Lord. Truly, you will be encouraged by her testimony of faith.

Black History

A Good Black Samaritan teaches biblical Black history—specifically how Jesus used people of color to teach the world what is good.